Perspectives on Kentucky's Past

ARCHITECTURE, ARCHAEOLOGY, AND LANDSCAPE

Julie Riesenweber
General Editor

The Synagogues of Kentucky

Architecture and History

Lee Shai Weissbach

THE UNIVERSITY PRESS OF KENTUCKY

Copyright © 1995 by The University Press of Kentucky

Scholarly publisher for the Commonwealth,
serving Bellarmine College, Berea College, Centre
College of Kentucky, Eastern Kentucky University,
The Filson Club, Georgetown College, Kentucky
Historical Society, Kentucky State University,
Morehead State University, Murray State University,
Northern Kentucky University, Transylvania University,
University of Kentucky, University of Louisville,
and Western Kentucky University.

Editorial and Sales Offices: Lexington, Kentucky 40508-4008

Library of Congress Cataloging-in-Publication Data

Weissbach, Lee Shai, 1947-
    The synagogues of Kentucky : architecture and history /
Lee Shai Weissbach.
        p.   cm. — (Perspectives on Kentucky's past)
    Includes bibliographical references and index.
    ISBN 0-8131-1912-X
    1. Synagogue architecture—Kentucky. 2. Synagogues—Kentucky.
I. Title. II. Series.
IN PROCESS
726'.3'09769—dc20   94-38736

This book is printed on acid-free recycled paper meeting
the requirements of the American National Standard
for Permanence of Paper for Printed Library Materials.

For Cobi and Maya

Contents

Maps

Sponsor's Foreword

KENTUCKY'S THOUSANDS OF CULTURAL resources form a tangible record of twelve thousand years of history and prehistory. They include archaeological sites such as native American villages and burial mounds, the historic remains of fortifications of our first European settlers, and Civil War earthworks and battlefields. Above ground are structures ranging from individual houses to entire streetscapes of Victorian commercial buildings. These resources combine to form a past and present environment—a cultural landscape—worthy of preservation.

Preservationists have always made decisions about which cultural resources should remain for future generations, but these decisions are becoming even more difficult. No longer is preservation a simple matter of saving old buildings from the wrecking ball or restoring them to their original appearance. Preservationists today must not only consider a more comprehensive and diverse array of properties, but also attempt to unravel the complex relationships among them. One way the profession responds to challenges posed by the rapidly changing times is to seek better understanding of the cultural resources with which it is concerned.

The Kentucky Heritage Council, the State Historic Preservation Office, encourages the study of the Commonwealth's architecture, archaeology, and landscape. As a growing number of constituents demand that decisions be weighed in light of many special interests, preservation increasingly becomes a public endeavor. The preservation profession must find ways of communicating the information gained through scholarly research so that the public is aware of the relationships and meanings behind practical decisions. Publication of the series Perspectives on Kentucky's Past is among the Kentucky Heritage Council's ongoing educational efforts.

Cultural diversity has become a major theme in many endeavors, including historic preservation. Where historical scholarship used to focus on rich and powerful white men, it now seeks information about working people, women and ethnic minorities in the past. Likewise, while early preservation efforts involved the restoration of masterworks of architecture and the stylish homes of prominent citizens, they now concern buildings, neighborhoods, communities and landscapes that were commonplace in the past and illustrate the diversity of American culture.

For this reason I am especially pleased that the second volume in the Perspectives on Kentucky's Past series presents information about an ethnic group not typically thought of in connection with Kentucky. *The Synagogues of Kentucky* is the first comprehensive survey of Kentucky's Jewish communities and synagogues. In this pioneering study of small Jewish communities outside the major American urban centers, Lee Shai Weissbach has employed demographic, architectural, and archival data and combined the disciplines of religious, social, and architectural history. He shows that synagogues, as the centers of Jewish religious and community life, have both influenced and reflected the evolution and identity of Jewish communal life in Kentucky, and he thus gives us persuasive reasons for their preservation.

David L. Morgan, Director
Kentucky Heritage Council and
State Historic Preservation Officer

Acknowledgments

IN PREPARING THIS VOLUME I have relied on the help of many individuals. Some made practical suggestions; others shared information and advice in correspondence or in conversation; still others assisted with the technical aspects of my project. I thank them all and offer my genuine apologies to anyone whose help I received but whom I have inadvertently failed to recognize here. It goes without saying, of course, that any faults to be found in this book are my responsibility alone.

My research could not have been accomplished without access to a great many primary sources, and at each and every one of the libraries and archives that I used (they are enumerated in my essay on methodology and bibliography), I found staff members who were extremely gracious and cooperative. Special mention in this regard is due to Kevin Proffitt of the American Jewish Archives in Cincinnati. Although I do not know by name all the other librarians and archivists who facilitated my research, I want to express my gratitude to them as a group.

Within each of the individual Kentucky communities I studied, I encountered many individuals who were willing and even eager to help me. For sharing their knowledge of the Louisville Jewish community and of their own congregations, I thank Herman Landau, the author of *Adath Louisville;* Milton Russman of the Israel T. Naamani Library located at Louisville's Jewish Community Center; Mary Wolf, one of the founders of the new Adat B'nai Yisrael congregation; Rabbi Chester Diamond of The Temple, and Jack Benjamin, The Temple's administrator. I also thank Richard Wolf, co-chair of the original building committee for The Temple; Rabbis Avrohom Litvin and Solomon Roodman of Congregation Anshei Sfard; Rabbi Shmuel Mann of Congregation Keneseth Israel; Rabbi Robert Slosberg of Adath Jeshurun; and Ernie Marks, that congregation's ritual director. I am indebted as well to the late Rabbi Simcha Kling of Adath Jeshurun, a native of the Newport Jewish community who became a highly revered communal leader and spiritual presence in Louisville; I regret that he did not live to see this volume completed.

Also deserving of my thanks are Louisville architects Gerald Baron, John P. Chovan, and Robert A. Nolan, Sr., each of whom spent time talking to me about his work on Kentucky's synagogues. I am grateful too for the aid and encouragement I received from Samuel W. Thomas, author of several books on Louisville's architectural environment, and from Joanne Weeter, my principal contact at the Louisville Landmarks Commission.

Beyond the city of Louisville my requests for help were amiably accommodated by Richard C. Brown of Danville, who attempted to find out as much as he could locally about the short-lived Jewish congregation in his town; Sonny Gergely, one of the last Jewish residents of Harlan, Kentucky; and Jennie Sable, one of the last Jewish residents of Hopkinsville. Several members of the now defunct Newport Jewish community also provided information and assistance: Morris Weintraub, now of Ft. Lauderdale, Florida; George Rosen, now of Cincinnati, Ohio; and Gordon Schilmeister, also of Cincinnati. Phyllis Schiff of Ft. Thomas, Kentucky, has done some of her own research on northern Kentucky Jewry, and I thank her for so willingly sharing her findings with me.

My sincere gratitude goes also to Robert Kaplan, Paul Bugay, and Adolph Baker of Owensboro's Adath Israel, and to Theodor Hirsch and Tod Megibow of Paducah's Temple Israel for helping me learn about their respective congregations. Jonathan Jeffrey of Western Kentucky University has done extensive research on Brinton B. Davis, the architect of the temple erected in Paducah in 1893, and I thank him for allowing me to consult his unpublished manuscript on Davis's career. For information about the Jewish community of Ashland, I relied heavily on Harold Freedman, Saul Kaplan, and Marty Weill, all of whom live in the Ashland area. For help with my work on Lexington, I want to recognize Rabbi Eric Slaton of Ohavay Zion, and Steve Caller, who was co-chair of that congregation's building committee when its present synagogue was constructed.

Over the past fifteen years or so, the Hillel Jewish Student Center at the University of Cincinnati has become an important repository for artifacts from synagogues that have been vacated all over the country, and items from several Kentucky congregations have found their way into its collection. The moving force behind the center's effort to recover and preserve items from abandoned synagogues is the current Hillel director there, Rabbi Abie Ingber. I offer him my sincere thanks not only for allowing me access to the Kentucky materials in the center's collection but also for his enthusiastic interest in my project.

In the course of my research I visited all of Kentucky's currently functioning synagogues and all the former synagogue buildings still standing in the commonwealth. Whenever I requested permission to roam around inside these buildings and take pictures, I encountered congenial people who often went out of their way to facilitate my work. Among those who assisted in my investigations of former synagogue buildings, I especially want to mention Elder Eugene Stewart of the Greater Bethel Apostolic Church in Louisville and Pastor Russel East of the Christ Corner Church in Henderson. Unfortunately, I did not learn the names of all the synagogue and church secretaries, maintenance workers, and congregants I met during my fieldwork, but I convey my heartfelt thanks to all of them nonetheless.

Any historian who holds an appointment at an academic institution benefits tremendously from being a part of a community of scholars, and I am pleased to be able to acknowledge the support and encouragement I received from so many people at the University of Louisville. Several colleagues in the Department of History provided valuable observations about my synagogue project, and the members of the department's office staff were always ready to do whatever they could to help. Katherine Burger Johnson, my research assistant for part of the time I was at work on this volume, also made valuable contributions.

For their assistance with photographic materials, I am indebted to James C. Anderson and Bill Carner of the University of Louisville Photographic Archives; to Dennis Robinson, Tom Fougerousse, and the late William Carlin of Information Technology at the university; and to Mary Jean Kinsman, curator of photographs and prints at the Filson Club in Louisville. For his excellent cartographic work I thank Steve Durban. Many of the captions to pictures in this volume identify a source; unattributed photographs are ones I took myself.

As this book project was nearing completion, I was very fortunate to find three colleagues who were willing to take the time to review preliminary drafts of the manuscript. They are William Morgan of the Fine Arts Department at the University of Louisville, Richard Cohen of the Hebrew University of Jerusalem, and Jack Wertheimer of the Jewish Theological Seminary of America in New York. Their insightful comments were most valuable, and I am extremely grateful to them.

I am very pleased that this volume has found a place in the Kentucky Heritage Council's series Perspectives on Kentucky's Past, and I thank Julie Riesenweber, general editor of the series, for her support. I also wish to thank all those who made my work with the University Press of Kentucky so pleasant and rewarding.

Several funding agencies provided financial support to help with my research on Kentucky's synagogues and with the publication of this volume. I want to acknowledge the assistance of the Kentucky Humanities Council and the National Endowment for the Humanities, the Southern Jewish Historical Society, and the Office of Research and Graduate Programs of the University of Louisville.

Finally, I want to express my gratitude to my wife, Sharon, for her love and encouragement as I pursued my study of the synagogues of the commonwealth. She was always a good listener when I needed a reaction to some idea about content or organization, and she has proved to be not only an ideal life's companion but a perceptive critic as well.

I have dedicated this volume to my children, Jacob ("Cobi") and Maya, who have contributed to its realization in their own special way. Because they are growing up as Jewish youngsters in Kentucky, they have come to know intimately some of the congregations and buildings described in this book. In a very profound sense, Kentucky's synagogues have left their mark on my children. By the same token, however, the association Cobi and Maya have had with several of Kentucky's synagogues has helped to shape the history and character of those institutions as well.

Introduction

SOMETIME IN THE SUMMER of 1842 a group of Jewish men assembled in Louisville, probably in one of the upper-floor rooms of Tandler's boardinghouse on Market Street, where they normally met for prayer services. The men who got together a few blocks from the Ohio River that summer's day discussed the recent growth of their little company of worshipers and decided that it was time to formalize the structure of their group and to seek a charter from the state. The formal recognition for which these early Louisvillians applied was granted on September 11, 1842, and the group adopted a set of bylaws on January 12, 1843. Thus was born Kentucky's first Jewish congregation, which the founders of the assembly named Adath Israel, the Congregation of Israel.[1]

The kind of scene played out on Market Street in 1842 was to be repeated many times in later years, not only in Louisville but in a number of other cities and towns throughout Kentucky as well. We have a detailed account, for example, of a similar meeting that took place in November 1903. This time the site of the gathering was a rented lodge hall on Short Street in downtown Lexington, where a dozen of the city's most prominent Jewish residents met to hold services, listen to the lecture of a visiting rabbi, and set in motion the establishment of a new congregation that they too would call Adath Israel.[2]

In January of 1931 a group of Jews from the towns of southeastern Kentucky got together to discuss the organization of communal life in their part of the state. These men met in the Masonic Hall at Middlesboro and inaugurated the B'nai Sholom congregation, which for the next

Figure 1. The cornerstone of Covington's first Temple of Israel building, begun in 1915 and occupied in 1916. The incorporation of this stone into the second Temple of Israel synagogue, begun in 1938, reflects the congregation's attachment to its early home. The Hebrew date on this cornerstone is 5676.

four decades was to center its activities in Harlan and serve the needs of Jewish families not only in that city and in Middlesboro but also in Pineville, Corbin, and several other small mountain towns as well.[3]

All together, there have been over two dozen occasions during the last century and a half when groups of Jews have gathered to create new congregations in Kentucky. The appearance of each one of these congregations was an important milestone in Kentucky's Jewish history, for the creation of each of these bodies marked the expansion of Jewish life in the commonwealth.

Sooner or later, most of the congregations that were founded in Kentucky acquired buildings of their own, and these synagogues inevitably became closely identified with the congregations they housed. As if to demonstrate their intimate connections with their buildings, those congregations that in due course moved from one synagogue to another nearly always took with them architectural reminders of their former homes. When Covington's Temple of Israel built its second sanctuary in 1938, for example, it not only laid a new cornerstone but also incorporated the cornerstone from its original synagogue into the foundation of its new one (see Figure 1). Similarly, when Louisville's Anshei Sfard congregation erected its new suburban sanctuary in 1964, it embedded in the building's front wall a section from the facade of the downtown synagogue it had abandoned (see Figure 2). When Lexington's Ohavay Zion moved from its old meeting place to its new building in 1986, the congregation brought along not only several plaques and ornaments (see Figure 3) but the pews from its original assembly hall as well. At

Figure 2. An architectural element from the 1928 facade of the Anshei Sfard synagogue on First Street in Louisville. This section of the old downtown building is embedded in the exterior wall of the new Anshei Sfard building on Dutchmans Lane.

Paducah's Temple Israel, too, the congregation has incorporated articles from its previous synagogue into its current sanctuary (see Figure 4).

Even though Jewish institutional life in America has not been focused solely upon the synagogue—as it once was in the Old World, where the synagogue and the community were more or less synonymous—the creation of religious institutions and the establishment of places of worship have long been hallmarks of Jewish communal life in the United States. Jack Wertheimer, an important contemporary commentator on American synagogue history, has singled out synagogues as "the oldest, hardiest and most participatory institutions maintained by Jews in the United States."[4] Even where Jews established other local institutions to deal with education, welfare, and cultural concerns, synagogues remained essential to Jewish communal life, and they often served many functions beyond providing services of a purely religious nature. This was especially true in smaller Jewish communities, where the synagogue was likely to be the only firmly established local Jewish institution, and where it could provide a setting for a wide variety of functions, even if some of them were not official congregational activities. During the 1920s in Newport, Kentucky, for example, the address of the United Hebrew Congregation's synagogue was also used by the

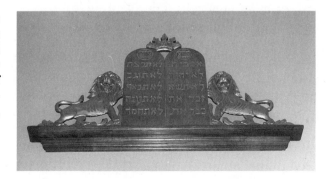

Figure 3. Lions from the interior of the Ohavay Zion synagogue on Maxwell Street in Lexington, now adorning the sanctuary of the new Ohavay Zion building on Edgewater Court.

Figure 4. The interior of Paducah's Temple Israel as it appeared in the early 1990s. The eternal light hanging before the ark (a standard feature in every synagogue), the tablets over the ark, and the menorahs on the wall are from Temple Israel's 1893 sanctuary.

Newport Zionist Society, which supported the creation of a Jewish homeland in Palestine, and by the Hebrew Emergency Association, the local Jewish community's main charitable organization.[5] Certainly it would be impossible to understand the Jewish experience in Kentucky without considering the history of the commonwealth's Jewish congregations and their synagogue buildings.

Because synagogue life has been of such great importance to the Jews of Kentucky, examining the history of the commonwealth's synagogues can provide many insights into the Jewish experience in Kentucky more generally. For example, we can learn a lot about the origins and the development of Kentucky's individual Jewish communities simply by studying when and where particular congregations and their houses of worship were established. Of course, a great deal of information about the emergence and fate of specific Jewish communities can be derived directly from data on Jewish population, and it makes sense to begin any examination of Jewish communal life in Kentucky by considering population figures such as those presented in Table 1, page 149. But population data alone do not reveal much about the development of communal structure or about the evolution of religious activity.

A complete understanding of the changing patterns of Jewish life in Kentucky can be gained only when information about population is considered in conjunction with other information, especially about communal institutions. The appearance of a congregation in Louisville as early as 1842, for example, serves as an indication that the Jews of the commonwealth's main urban center were already creating a communal infrastructure quite early in the nineteenth century. By the same token, the fact that there were synagogue buildings standing in three other towns besides Louisville when the commonwealth celebrated its centennial in 1892 makes it clear that the state's largest city was not its only center of Jewish religious and cultural life (see Map 1). Indeed, less than half of Kentucky's Jewish congregations have been located in Louisville over the last 150 years.

The appearance of new synagogues in Louisville around the turn of the twentieth century and the creation of new congregations in Ashland, Newport, Covington, and elsewhere point to yet another development in the history of Kentucky Jewry. The proliferation of Kentucky synagogues in the half-century before World War II reflects the massive migration of East European Jews to America in the decades after 1881 and suggests that this migration had a profound impact on the nature of Jewish life in the commonwealth. The arrival of East European Jews not only significantly increased the size of Kentucky's Jewish population but also altered the pattern of Jewish settlement (see Map 2) and transformed the internal structure of organized Jewish life in the state. Additional synagogues went up in Kentucky not only because the state's Jewish population was growing but also because it was becoming more diverse in its approach to religious issues.

Just as the appearance of new congregations around the turn of the century reflected the impact of immigration on Jewish life in Kentucky, the disappearance of Jewish congregations from Henderson, Harlan, Hopkinsville, and several other towns helps tell the story of the departure of Jewish families from Kentucky's smaller communities in more recent decades. The advent of interstate highways, chain stores, and shopping malls has eliminated many of the economic opportunities that kept the Jewish merchant families of Kentucky's smaller cities in business, and the withdrawal of these families is reflected in the decline of organized Jewish life in several small towns (see Map 3).

Of course, helping to chart changing patterns of Jewish settlement is only one way in which the history of Kentucky's Jewish congregations and their synagogues can allow us to learn about Kentucky's Jewish history in general. If we can come to understand the specific reasons for the establishment of Kentucky's various congregations, if we can acquaint ourselves with the philosophical considerations that helped to mold their identities, and if we can analyze why Kentucky's synagogue buildings looked the way they did, we will be able to discover much

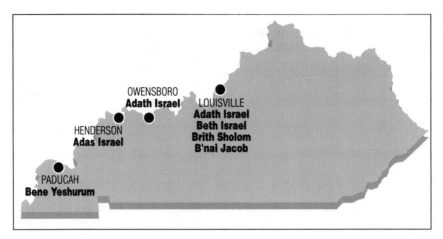

Map 1. Synagogue buildings in Kentucky in 1892.

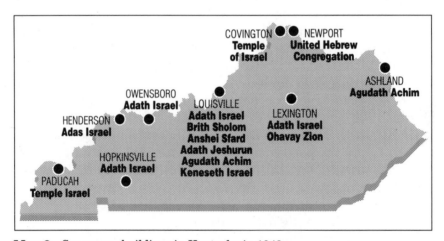

Map 2. Synagogue buildings in Kentucky in 1942.

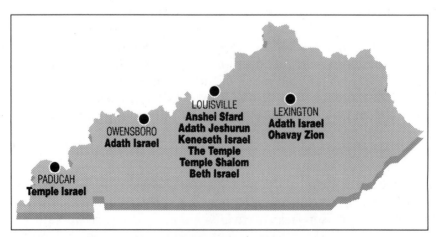

Map 3. Synagogue buildings in Kentucky in 1992.

about the religious practices of Kentucky Jews, about the social structure of their communities, and even about certain aspects of their
collective mentality.

As the data in Table 1 indicate, Kentucky has never had a very
large Jewish population. Around 1878 the 3,600 Jews living in the state
represented only about 1.5 percent of the state's total population, and a
mere two-tenths of 1 percent of all the Jews in the United States. Even
sixty years later, when the arrival of East European immigrants had
swelled the Jewish population of the United States to nearly 5 million,
the total number of Jews in Kentucky was still only about 18,000.
Nonetheless, the history of Kentucky Jewry is of considerable interest,
for over the decades Jewish congregations have enriched the religious
milieu of a dozen Kentucky cities, and the synagogues these congregations occupied have added variety and distinctiveness to the architectural landscape of several of the commonwealth's urban centers.
Moreover, it is only by taking into account the experience of the commonwealth's minority groups that the richness and the diversity of
Kentucky's ethnic, cultural, and religious heritage can be fully appreciated.

In much the same way, Kentucky's Jewish history is of importance
to the story of American Jewry. Scholars working in the field of American Jewish history have until now paid very little attention to Jewish
life outside the major centers of Jewish population in the United States.
They have virtually ignored the less conspicuous Jewish communities
that have dotted the American landscape over the last century and a
half, for the most part basing their accounts of American Jewish history
on developments in the nation's largest cities. There is a particular
paucity of information about Jewish life in those cities and towns where
the Jewish population never rose beyond a few hundred or perhaps a
couple of thousand. This is unfortunate, for it is only by considering the
history of smaller and more remote Jewish communities that the American Jewish experience can be understood in all its splendor and com-
plexity.

The significance of Kentucky's Jewish heritage both for the history
of the commonwealth and for the history of American Jewry makes it
essential to preserve as much knowledge as possible about Jewish life in
the Bluegrass State. Given the centrality of congregational life in the
Jewish experience, it is especially important to know something about
Kentucky's Jewish congregations and about the tangible symbols of
those congregations, their synagogue buildings. Until now, no comprehensive survey of the commonwealth's Jewish congregations and synagogues has ever been undertaken. This volume is the result of the very
first such effort, and its specific purposes are threefold: to provide ready
access to basic information about the history of Kentucky's Jewish
congregations and their houses of worship; to examine Kentucky's syna-

gogue buildings both in the context of the American Jewish experience and as a part of the commonwealth's architectural heritage; and to create a visual record of the synagogue buildings that have served the Jewish communities of the commonwealth over the last century and a half.

Although this book explores what is arguably the most elemental aspect of Kentucky's Jewish history, it should be emphasized that it is not intended to be an intensive examination of the history of each of Kentucky's individual Jewish congregations, much less a complete account of the Jewish experience in the commonwealth in all its dimensions. A full discussion of each of Kentucky's congregations would have to consider several very large questions that this volume does not address. It would have to examine exactly who established the various congregations, who joined them, and who supported them. It would have to consider the internal dynamics of each congregation and each congregation's interaction with other institutions in its environment. It would also have to explore in great detail the changing functions of each congregation over time.

A complete history of Kentucky Jewry would have to go even further. It would have to investigate such subjects as family life, occupational patterns, political involvements, and social relations. It would have to recognize the many Jewish personalities who have played a role in Kentucky history. And it would have to consider the dozens of Jewish educational, philanthropic, and social organizations that functioned alongside congregations over the years. At the end of World War I, for example, there were at least a dozen Jewish charitable societies and half a dozen Jewish educational organizations in Louisville alone.[6] A complete study of the Jews in Kentucky would also have to take into account sites of Jewish interest besides synagogue buildings. Throughout the state scores of homes, places of business, schools, and cemeteries have been connected with the history of Kentucky Jewry in one way or another. Although this book does relate the history of Kentucky's Jewish congregations and synagogues to several fundamental themes in the study of Jewish history, its primary goals remain much more limited. In a sense, it might be seen as a first step toward a much fuller investigation of the history of Jewish life in the commonwealth.

In order to fulfill its specific purposes, I have built this book around several components. The first of these is the text. Chapter 1 examines the formation of Kentucky's individual Jewish congregations and briefly reviews their history, while Chapters 2, 3, and 4 present an inventory of the synagogue buildings that have served Kentucky Jewry over the past 150 years and discuss these buildings as a part of Kentucky's built environment and American Jewry's material culture. The text alludes frequently to the tables I have prepared to summarize much of the information amassed for this study, and these tables are the second main component of the book, presented as a separate section for ease of reference. The pictorial material is yet another major component and, in many ways, the book's heart and soul.

The information presented in the text and tables of this volume emerged only after I had consulted a great many references and reconciled their many ambiguities and contradictions. Indeed, as I worked on this project, it occurred to me that how the research for this book was conducted is a significant story in itself. And so I have included in this volume an essay, "Discovering Kentucky's Synagogues," in which I discuss the sources from which I extracted data and explain the process by which I compiled information. Because I realized that I could document the evidentiary base on which this study rests much more clearly and usefully in an essay on sources and methodology than I could with a profusion of reference notes, I have employed individual citations only where direct quotations are involved or where particular sources deserve special mention.

In this book, I have endeavored to reconstruct the basic story of Kentucky's Jewish congregations and their synagogues as accurately as possible, and I have sought to create a pictorial record of Kentucky Jewry's houses of worship that is both comprehensive in its coverage and enlightening in its content. My hope is that this volume will both make a contribution to the field of American Jewish history and increase public awareness of Kentucky's rich Jewish heritage. It is also my wish that this review of Kentucky synagogues will help draw attention to the significance of smaller Jewish communities throughout America and perhaps serve as a model for inventories of Jewish congregations and synagogues in other parts of the country.

Although this volume deals with the congregations and synagogues of only one particular geographic region, it does address some general questions about the proliferation of Jewish congregations, about congregational naming patterns, about the financing of synagogue construction and the selection of architects, and about numerous other matters relating to synagogue history. To the extent that it answers these questions in the context of Kentucky's Jewish experience, it also provides clues about the way small and medium-size Jewish communities have functioned throughout the United States. Information about Jewish communal infrastructure and the Jewish built environment is essential to an understanding of Jewish life at the local level, and this study demonstrates that even for regions with very small Jewish populations (or perhaps especially for such regions), accurate and systematic surveys of congregational and synagogue history are not only feasible but highly rewarding.

Chapter 1

The Formation of Kentucky's Jewish Congregations

FROM THE PERSPECTIVE of Jewish tradition, very little is required in order for a group of individuals to organize for public worship. Jewish practice does not require that prayer services be conducted with the participation of a rabbi, or within a synagogue building, or with the sanction of any hierarchical authority. Traditionally, the only fundamental requirement for Jewish public worship has been the presence of a *minyan*, a quorum of ten adult men, and in recent times even that requirement has been modified within some communities. Today, in some circles, women may be counted in the *minyan*, or the standards for defining a minimum number of worshipers may be ignored altogether. Since public readings from the Torah, the Five Books of Moses, form an integral part of Sabbath and holiday services, and since the Torah scroll is the focus of much religious ritual, the presence of this sacred object might also be considered a necessity for public worship. There is nothing in Jewish custom, however, that would prevent any group of individuals who wanted a Torah scroll from acquiring one.

Moreover, even though in other times and in other places local authorities both outside and inside the Jewish community have exerted a great deal of control over Jewish communal organization, in the United States over the last two centuries, Jews have enjoyed an almost complete freedom to organize their religious lives and their communal institutions however they have seen fit. Thus, in Kentucky as in other places where Jews have settled in the United States, any assembly of Jews that wished to establish itself formally as a congregation usually has been able to do so without encountering any inherent difficulties.

The ease with which both Jewish tradition and American society have allowed for the creation of congregational bodies helps explain why no fewer than thirty different Jewish congregations have come into existence in Kentucky since the middle of the nineteenth century.

The lack of institutional barriers to the formation of new congregations, however, is only one factor to be considered in telling the story of Jewish congregational organization in Kentucky. Certainly the proliferation of congregations in the commonwealth is also due in part to the fact that over the years Kentucky's Jewish citizens have distributed themselves rather widely throughout the state. The population figures presented in Table 1 make it clear that the largest concentration of Jews in the commonwealth has always been in Louisville, but the data also show that river towns such as Paducah, Owensboro, Covington, and Newport have had significant Jewish populations in the past as well. So have a few cities of the interior, notably Lexington and Hopkinsville. In each of these and a few other towns, Jewish assemblies have existed to serve the local community. All told, there are eleven different cities and towns in Kentucky where Jewish congregations have functioned at one time or another, though in some of these places organized Jewish life lasted only a short time (the prime example is that of Danville, where a local congregation functioned for only a couple of years in the late 1940s).

Another factor that helps account for the appearance of numerous Jewish congregations in Kentucky is the divergence of opinion among Jews over matters of religious belief and usage. Perhaps the central issue that has divided American Jewry since at least the middle of the nineteenth century concerns the alteration of traditional Jewish doctrines and practices in response to changing social environments. Disagreements over the maintenance of traditional beliefs and rituals has resulted in the segmentation of American Judaism into several branches. Orthodox Judaism, as it has come to be called, asserts that all Jewish practice is God-ordained, that it has the power of law, and that it is essentially immutable.

The Reform Judaism that developed in the nineteenth century, on the other hand, has come to treat the requirements of the Jewish legal code, the *halacha*, as mere custom, and it has abandoned many of the usages maintained in the Jewish faith for hundreds or even thousands of years. Conservative Judaism has taken a position somewhere between that of Orthodoxy and that of Reform. It accepts the binding character of *halacha* but tends to be somewhat lenient in its interpretation of Jewish law and rather flexible in recognizing its evolution. In very recent years the new designation Traditional has been adopted by some American Jewish congregations, denoting a position somewhere between that of Orthodoxy and that of Conservatism. Reconstructionist Judaism, occupying a place somewhere between Conservatism and

Reform, also exists as a variant of American Judaism, but it has never been officially represented in any of Kentucky's Jewish congregations.

Because American Judaism has become divided into various branches with different attitudes toward Jewish law, liturgical practices and ritual observances vary quite widely from congregation to congregation. In Orthodox assemblies, for instance, men and women sit separately; heads are covered; and the men generally wear prayer shawls at morning services. Orthodox services, which are primarily in Hebrew and unaccompanied by musical instruments, are conducted exclusively by males. In Reform congregations, by contrast, families sit together; heads may be bare; and the services, often accompanied by an organ and a choir, tend to be shortened and altered versions of older forms, frequently translated into English. In Conservative and Traditional congregations, much of the Orthodox liturgy is retained and there is no organ, but families sit together, and women may or may not participate in conducting worship services. While the centrality of Saturday morning worship has been maintained in Orthodox, Traditional, and Conservative congregations, Reform congregations have increasingly tended to hold their main Sabbath services on Friday evening. This is mainly because Reform Judaism has dropped the age-old prohibition of labor on the Sabbath and has recognized that for most American Jews, Saturday is no longer a day of rest reserved for prayer, study, and relaxation. In the past, some Reform congregations even experimented with a Sunday observance of the Sabbath.

Although it is very common to find that individual congregants do not adhere to the theological positions supported by their congregations, synagogue members have nonetheless always tended to believe that, as institutions, their congregations should identify closely with one or another of the various branches of American Judaism. Thus, even in rather small Jewish communities, a single congregational body has not always been able to cater to the requirements of all the local Jews, and this has created the need for additional assemblies. In Kentucky, the existence of two congregations side by side in both Lexington and Ashland was the result primarily of theological division rather than demographic pressure.

Besides population growth, statewide dispersal, and ideological distinctions, other factors also help explain the appearance of more than two dozen Jewish congregations in Kentucky. In a few cases the creation of a new congregation was the result of the restructuring and renaming of an older body. This was probably the case in Lexington, where the Adath Israel congregation organized at the beginning of the twentieth century seems to have taken over the congregational functions of the older Spinoza Society. Similarly, Adath Jeshurun in Louisville appears to have been a new and more liberal entity, following what today would be called Conservative practice, formed specifically to replace the Orthodox Beth Israel assembly that disbanded in 1894.

In America's larger Jewish communities throughout the nineteenth century and into the twentieth, the existence of various affinity groupings and social circles often helped account for the creation of new congregations. In Kentucky's largest city, too, internal social structure seems to have played a role in congregational formation; as early as the mid-nineteenth century, members of Adath Israel were already worried about "the possible admission to the congregation of an undesirable element."[1] The fact that two different Reform congregations and four different Orthodox bodies were functioning in Louisville during the 1920s can be explained only with some reference to factors that had little to do with practical considerations or basic disagreements over religious ideology.

One specific factor that often drew certain groups of individuals together to form their own congregations was their European place of origin. In Louisville, for example, it was Jews of Polish derivation who created the Beth Israel congregation in 1851. Beth Israel was actually chartered as "the Polish House of Israel," and as late as 1868 its place of worship was still identified in the Louisville city directory as the "Polish synagogue." Before 1851 Louisville's Polish Jews (most of whose roots were probably in the Prussian-controlled province of Posen) had been members of the city's Adath Israel congregation. But Adath Israel was dominated by Jews who hailed from western Germany, and although the founders of Beth Israel differed little from these German Jews in basic religious philosophy, they went their own way in order to perpetuate some of the specific local customs and liturgical nuances that they had brought with them from Europe.

The predilection of modern Jews to divide themselves into different congregations and then to develop fierce loyalties to their own assemblies while disdaining other bodies (even those located within their own communities and very similar in ideology and practice) is so much a feature of Jewish life that it has become a recurrent subject in Jewish humor. Perhaps the best-known joke on this theme is the one about the Jewish survivor of a shipwreck who spent several years on an uninhabited island. When he was finally discovered, the marooned Jew offered to take his rescuers on a tour so they could see how he had been living while waiting to be found. Over the years he had erected several rude structures out of materials available on the island: a dwelling, a workshop, a storehouse, a cabana by the beach, and two huts to serve as synagogues. "Why two synagogues?" asked the rescuers. "All these years you've been here completely alone." "Well," answered the shipwreck survivor, pointing to one of the huts, "this is the synagogue I go to, and the other is the one I wouldn't set foot in."

Table 2, page 150, provides a complete list of all the Jewish congregations that are known to have existed in Kentucky since Jewish settlement began in the state over a century and a half ago. The table is arranged chronologically by the date of each congregation's founding. As even a quick review of the table reveals, the congregations included are not only those well-established assemblies that functioned in the commonwealth's major cities over many decades but also less firmly rooted ones (such as the Blue Grass Judean Society of Danville) that lasted for only a few years and that may never have had a resident rabbi or a synagogue building of their own.

It should be noted, however, that Table 2 does not include informal associations that never organized officially or whose members assembled only occasionally to hold worship services. Not listed, for example, are two Louisville prayer groups that got as far as adopting names, but apparently did not survive for more than a few months; each appears only once in documentary sources. They are Shaar Hashomaim (Gate of Heaven), which is reported to have held services at the corner of Brook and Hill Streets in Old Louisville in the fall of 1931 for the High Holidays of Rosh Hashanah and Yom Kippur (the Jewish New Year and the Day of Atonement), and Machzikai Hados (Supporters of the Faith), which was listed in the 1932 Louisville city directory as meeting at the residence of Rabbi Asher Zarchy at 507 East Chestnut Street. Zarchy was for many years the most important Orthodox rabbi in the city, overseeing the Louisville Hebrew School and several congregations. It is likely that Machzikai Hados was a circle of worshipers that gathered around Zarchy in the final year of his life, and then disbanded.

Also not listed among Kentucky's Jewish congregations is the collection of families in Frankfort that for a time after World War II arranged annual Rosh Hashanah and Yom Kippur services. Similarly excluded is a small body of individuals who worshiped together on Saturday mornings at Louisville's Jewish day school in the 1950s and 1960s (they did so out of a desire to hold Orthodox services in the Highlands neighborhood at a time when most of Louisville's synagogues were still downtown). A northern Kentucky group that gathered once in a while to observe Jewish holidays during the early and middle 1980s is also absent from Table 2.[2] The thirty congregations that are included in Table 2 are listed again in Table 3, a city-by-city inventory prepared as an additional reference guide.

It has generally been the custom for Jewish congregations to choose Hebrew names for themselves, and Table 2 provides a translation of the name of every Kentucky congregation that had a Hebrew designation (in those cases where a congregation has generally been known by its English name, the Hebrew name appears in parentheses). Most of Kentucky's Jewish congregations chose names that were straightforwardly descriptive: Congregation of Israel, House of Israel,

Assembly of Israel. Others chose names that alluded to the values they sought to represent: peace, brotherhood, uprightness, scholarship.

The English word "temple" is found in the names of several Kentucky congregations, and for Reform Jews, at least, the use of this word has its origins in a specific theological tenet. Traditionally, the Jewish concept of Messianic times has included a vision of the ingathering of the Jewish people to its ancient homeland and the restoration of a central Temple in Jerusalem. Reform Judaism, which promoted the integration of Jews into the societies around them, rejected the concept of a redemption centered on the Land of Israel, however, and Reform congregations often adopted the use of the term "temple" in the names of their congregations and places of worship in order to emphasize that they had no longing for the restoration of a central Temple in the Holy Land. Reform Jews may also have preferred to use the term "temple" for their houses of prayer because it sounded less alien than the Greek word "synagogue." Some congregations that follow a more traditional variety of Judaism have used the word "temple" in their names as well—the Temple of Israel in Covington is an example—but this practice has not been common, and it has certainly been adopted without embracing the theological implications Reform Judaism had attached to it. In the case of Covington's congregation, the name "Temple of Israel" may have had its origin as a direct translation, perhaps not the best, of the Hebrew designation "Hechal Yisrael."

When they adopted their names, different congregations sometimes used variant spellings of the same Hebrew word. For example, the appellation "Adath Israel" was chosen by several Kentucky congregations, but in Henderson the form "Adas Israel" was always employed, and in Louisville's newest congregation the form "Adat Yisrael" is used. Similarly, the congregation in Paducah was know originally as Bene Yeshurum, but the two words constituting this name appear as "B'nai" and "Jeshurun" in the names of two Louisville congregations. The word for "lovers" appears as "Ohavay" in the name of Lexington's Ohavay Zion, but the same word is spelled "Ohave" in the name of Newport's Ohave Sholom. There are even cases where the same congregation spelled its name in different ways at different times: Louisville's Adath Israel and Adath Jeshurun were originally known as Adas Israel and Adas Jeshurun, and for many years Ohavay Zion's name was spelled "Ohava Zion."

There are several possible reasons for these variations in spelling. Different congregations may have transliterated their names in accordance with different dialects of Hebrew. This explains the distinction between "Adas" and "Adat," for example, and it is also why the word for peace is spelled "Sholom" in the names of three older Kentucky congregations, but "Shalom" in the more recently established Temple Shalom in Louisville. So too, different congregations may have spelled their names in conformity with different systems of transliteration. Or some may simply have made errors in transliteration, as seems to be the case in the designation "Bene Yeshurum," where the final consonant should have been an "n." In any event, congregational names are presented in this volume the way the congregations themselves most often spelled them. The Hebrew names of Newport's United Hebrew Congregation (Agudat Yisrael) and Covington's Temple of Israel (Hechal Yisrael) are known only in their Hebrew spellings, so standard modern Hebrew transliterations have been provided.

Along with translating congregational names, Table 2 also indicates the branch of Judaism with which each of Kentucky's congregations can be identified. Data about theological orientation is significant because, as we have seen, theological differences help account for the formation of several congregations, and also because decisions about religious affiliation often reflect the beliefs and lifestyles of the people who live within a specific community. The presence of an Orthodox congregation in a city or town suggests that there are at least some members of the local community who still feel that traditional Jewish practice should be maintained, who observe the Sabbath and the Jewish holidays in accordance with Jewish law, who "keep kosher" (observe the Jewish dietary laws), who worship on a regular basis, and who adhere in general to the precepts of the *halacha*. The presence of a Reform congregation, on the other hand, suggests that there are Jews in the local community who view much of traditional Jewish practice as superfluous and who prefer to identify with a variety of Judaism that places fewer ritual demands on their lives.

The predominance of Reform congregations in Kentucky's smaller Jewish communities is not surprising, given that it has always been difficult in such communities to find the resources and establish the support networks necessary to maintain a lifestyle that includes a strict adherence to Jewish law. Nor is it surprising that over the course of the twentieth century the number of Orthodox congregations in Kentucky has declined. As American Jews have gotten further and further removed from their immigrant origins, and as American society has become more open and inviting, Jews in the United States (especially where they do not live together in large concentrations) have tended to become more liberal in their religious ideologies and less willing to abide by the requirements of traditional Jewish practice.

The movement away from traditional practice is reflected in the fact that several of Kentucky's congregations have actually changed their religious philosophies over time. When it was established in the 1840s, for example, Louisville's first congregation, Adath Israel, was identified with Orthodoxy. Around the middle of the 1850s, however, the congregation began to adopt the philosophy and the rituals of Reform. One account concludes that Adath Israel is the seventh oldest Reform congregation in America.[3] The lone Jewish congregation in Paducah followed a similar path, beginning as an Orthodox body but turning toward Reform within a few years of its establishment.[4]

In Ashland, Agudath Achim was originally an Orthodox congregation, but around 1921 a majority of its members decided that the synagogue should become affiliated with Reform Judaism. It was then that the Orthodox minority in Ashland established the city's second congregation, the House of Israel.[5] Lexington's Ohavay Zion provides an example of a congregation that began as an Orthodox assembly and then became Conservative. Yet another example of changing affiliation comes from the recent history of Keneseth Israel in Louisville. Until just a few years ago this congregation was affiliated with the Union of Orthodox Jewish Congregations of America; then for several years it identified itself as a Traditional congregation; and in 1994 its members voted to join the organizational network of Conservative congregations.

In Table 2, the branch designation assigned each congregation indicates its original orientation and, if it changed its religious philosophy at some point, its subsequent affiliation as well. For any congregation that did not formally affiliate with the Reform, Conservative, or Orthodox umbrella organizations that have long functioned in the United States, the branch designation indicates the general tone of its religious philosophy.

Many of the Jewish congregations established in Kentucky began as casually assembled groups holding prayer services in temporary locations, and several of these seem to have functioned informally for some time before they organized themselves into regular congregations. For example, the founders of Louisville's Adath Israel had apparently been worshiping together for some six years before they held the 1842 meeting on Market Street at which they decided to seek a charter from the state, and it was 1849 before the congregation moved into its first synagogue building.

The Bene Yeshurum congregation in Paducah (later known as Temple Israel) also had something of a prehistory. It had its origins in the Chevra Yeshurum Burial Society, founded in 1859, which organized Paducah's first prayer services for the High Holidays of Rosh Hashanah and Yom Kippur in 1868; they were held in a third-floor hall over the downtown store of M. Livingston and Company, a firm owned by one of Paducah's most prominent Jewish families. The burial society did not change its name and formally constitute itself a congregation until 1871.[6]

In Lexington, too, the first Jewish congregation evolved from a preexisting association. In 1872 a group of twenty-eight men established the Spinoza Burial Society, named, rather curiously, in honor of the seventeenth-century Dutch Jewish thinker Baruch Spinoza, who had been banned from the Amsterdam Jewish community. Perhaps the founders of the society admired Spinoza's rationalist philosophy. In any case, by 1877 it was clear that the Spinoza Society (sometimes referred to as the Spinoza Association) was destined to do much more than simply oversee the interment of the Jewish dead in central Kentucky. In a quaintly worded resolution introduced in October of 1877, Moses Kaufman, one of Lexington's leading citizens, noted that it was "the expressed wish of the Israelites of this City . . . that a Jewish Congregation be organized in this place." Observing that "all the Israelites [of Lexington] are also Members of the Spinoza Association," Kaufman argued that "it is an unheard of thing and contrary to all custom, usage, rule and harmony, that a Congregation and a burial association, both wholly composed of members of the same faith and organization, should exist apart from each other in the same place." In a move that won the unanimous approval of the members of the Spinoza Society, Kaufman then proposed that "besides burying the dead for which this society was solely at first organized, it is to form also a Jewish Congregation."[7]

Toward the end of the nineteenth century, a major turning point in the institutional life of Kentucky Jewry arrived. Since midcentury the Jews of Eastern Europe had been suffering the effects of growing economic hardship, urban crowding, and unemployment. In addition, following the assassination of Tsar Alexander II of Russia in 1881, a climate of tremendous repression and anti-Semitic violence took hold in Eastern Europe. As a result, hundreds of thousands of East European Jews sought refuge in America in the final two decades of the nineteenth century and in the early years of the twentieth. The mass migration of East European Jews had a profound impact on Jewish life in Kentucky, just as it had on Jewish life elsewhere in the United States. The effects of migration can be seen most graphically, perhaps, in population growth. In the fifty years after 1881, Louisville's Jewish population grew from less than 3,000 to more than 12,000, and the Jewish populations of several other Kentucky towns mounted dramatically as well.

With the growth of Kentucky's Jewish population came a striking increase in the number of Jewish congregations in the state. Between 1881 and 1910 a dozen new congregational bodies were established, and five more had been added by 1931. Because nearly all these new congregations were organized by immigrants from Eastern Europe or their children, they were predominantly traditional in their orientation. Among East European Jews, religious practice had always been based on *halacha*, because those who rejected Orthodoxy generally turned toward secularism rather than toward some liberalized form of religious observance. Reform Judaism was essentially unknown in Eastern Europe, and it had little appeal to the new immigrants arriving in America. By the turn of the twentieth century, most of Kentucky's oldest congregations (the Adath Israel congregations of Louisville and

Owensboro, for example, and Temple Israel of Paducah) had turned toward Reform, and so the formation of new congregations was a function not only of increasing population pressure but also of the need for assemblies with a traditional orientation. Of the seventeen congregations established in Kentucky between 1881 and 1931, twelve were organized as Orthodox assemblies, three as Conservative bodies, and only two as Reform congregations.

Most of the new congregations that came into being in the decades after 1881, like the commonwealth's very earliest Jewish assemblies, began as informal associations, and most conducted their activities in temporary facilities during their earliest years. Indeed, while they were getting started, the new congregations sometimes found themselves moving from one location to another rather frequently. A case in point is Beth Hamedrash Hagodol, an Orthodox assembly founded in Louisville in 1887.[8]

It is not known where Beth Hamedrash Hagodol first held services, but the Louisville city directory for 1891 shows the congregation as one of the tenants in a Jefferson Street building that had previously housed the butcher shop of Louis Warskansky. By 1893, however, that building had become the site of a physician's office, and Beth Hamedrash Hagodol had moved into a former machine shop on Floyd Street. Two years later the former machine shop had become a laboratory, and Beth Hamedrash Hagodol had moved a few doors down into a building that also housed a bakery.

By 1896 the members of Beth Hamedrash Hagodol seem to have begun holding services in a one-story structure at 425 East Jefferson Street which also served as the schoolhouse of Azariah Epstein. Between 1898 and 1900 the assembly that met at this address was listed in the Louisville city directory as the Talmud Torah Congregation. It is possible that this was a newly formed body, but given that Beth Hamedrash Hagodol is not listed at all in the city directories of 1898, 1899, and 1900, it is much more probable that Beth Hamedrash Hagodol was simply misidentified in the directories for several years. "Talmud Torah" is a term denoting a Jewish school, and some confusion may have resulted from the fact that both a school and a congregational meeting place were located at the same site. It is more than likely that the Talmud Torah congregation and Beth Hamedrash Hagodol were one and the same institution.

In any case, in 1901 Beth Hamedrash Hagodol reemerged as the name of the assembly meeting at 425 East Jefferson, and the congregation remained there until 1905, when it moved to the grounds of the former St. Paul's German Lutheran Church. For three years the congregation used as its address that of a single-story dwelling on Green Street, at the rear of St. Paul's Church, and it was probably during this period that the church itself was renovated for use as a synagogue (see

Figure 5). Thus, only in 1908, some twenty years after its founding, did Beth Hamedrash Hagodol find itself housed in a building that could unquestionably be called a synagogue (see Figure 6).

Anshei Sfard, another of Louisville's Orthodox congregations, had a similarly peripatetic start. According to city directories from the turn of the century, Anshei Sfard's address in 1897 and 1898 was that of a

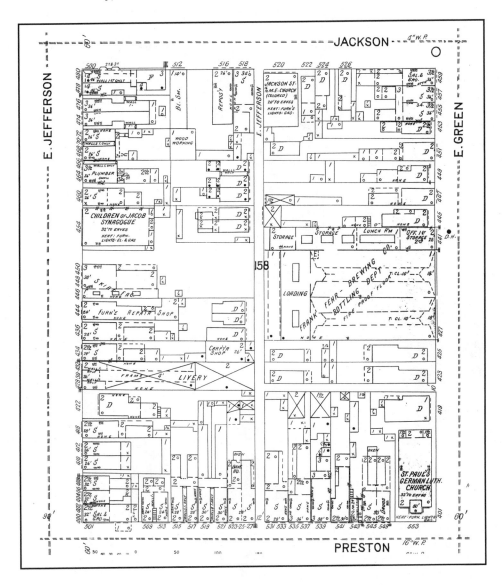

Figure 5. This portion of Sheet 161, Volume 2, of the 1905 Sanborn insurance map series for Louisville shows the St. Paul's German Lutheran Church at Preston and Green just before it was bought by Beth Hamedrash Hagodol. This map also shows the dwelling at 419 Green Street, at the rear of the St. Paul's property, that served as Beth Hamedrash Hagodol's home for a short time, and the B'nai Jacob synagogue building dedicated in 1901 at 454 East Jefferson Street (later designated 432 East Jefferson).

dwelling occupied by Jacob Brownstein, located between a boarding-house and a hook-and-ladder station on Eighth Street. The congregation then met for several years in a three-story building at 716 West Walnut Street, which housed not only a school run by Benjamin Seligman but also a number of other tenants (for one year at least, they included the spiritual leader of B'nai Jacob, a rival Orthodox congregation). Anshei Sfard remained in the three-story building on Walnut

Figure 6. Beth Hamedrash Hagodol, Preston Street, Louisville. The Orthodox Beth Hamedrash Hagodol congregation took over this former Lutheran church in 1905. When Keneseth Israel was formed by the merger of Beth Hamedrash Hagodol and B'nai Jacob, the young congregation used this building until it occupied its new sanctuary in 1929. The building is shown here as it appeared in 1941. From the University of Louisville Photographic Archives, Caufield and Shook Collection (neg. 182495).

Street until 1903, when it purchased the synagogue on First Street (Figure 22) that had until then been the home of the older Brith Sholom congregation.

Because Jewish law restricts travel on the Sabbath, Orthodox Jews have always had to locate their places of worship within walking distance of their homes, and for many years the Anshei Sfard congregation had served the needs of religiously observant Jews at the western end of downtown Louisville. Thus, when Anshei Sfard moved to its First Street location, it created a void in its old neighborhood. It was almost certainly for this reason that the Agudath Achim congregation was organized around 1905. Following what had become a typical pattern, the congregation held its services in temporary locations for several years. Between 1912 and 1916 the assembly met at the Odd Fellows hall on West Walnut Street at Sixth, for example, and only in 1917 did Agudath Achim finally move into a building of its own, the former St. John's

Figure 7. Agudath Achim, Jefferson Street, Louisville. This building, originally St. John's Episcopal Church, became the home of the Agudath Achim congregation in 1917. Photo courtesy of Keneseth Israel Congregation.

Episcopal Church on West Jefferson Street near Eleventh (see Figure 7).

In Kentucky's smaller cities, as in Louisville, newly formed congregations also commonly used temporary quarters in their earliest years. In Henderson, Adas Israel met above a bakery on the town's Main Street and in the second floor Liederkranz Hall at the corner of Second and Elm Streets until it moved into its own sanctuary in 1892 (Figure 23). In Covington, the Temple of Israel congregation met in the Kentucky Post Building on Madison Avenue in its earliest years. Then, between the time it vacated its first synagogue (Figure 38) and the time its second building was constructed (Figure 41), it used temporary facilities in the local Odd Fellows building. In Ashland, both of the city's congregations met in buildings on Greenup Street, a major downtown thoroughfare, before they built their respective synagogue buildings in 1938 and 1947 (Figures 42 and 60).[9]

It was almost certainly a lack of financial resources that kept most congregations from settling into their own facilities in their early years. Fund raising for a building was often a major effort for a congregation, and it generally depended on marshaling the resources of many individuals. A detailed report on the funds solicited for the building of Covington's first synagogue early in the twentieth century is instructive in this regard. It reveals that by the beginning of 1915, Meyer Berman, the president of the congregation, had given $100 toward construction costs, and that the Levine brothers, who were also officers of the congregation, had given an equivalent sum. Beyond these contributors to the building fund, there were ninety-five others, both individuals and businesses, almost all of whom made donations of between $5.00 and $25.00.[10]

Several congregations raised funds by selling seats or pews to members (or, perhaps more correctly, selling the right to occupy seats or pews). The most desirable places, usually toward the front of the sanctuary, commanded the highest prices. As a result, the wealthiest members of a congregation were often the ones seated most conspicuously in the synagogue. When Louisville's Adath Israel built its first sanctuary in the late 1840s, it was resolved that every member of the congregation had to buy a pew at auction, the minimum purchase price being $50. When the second Adath Israel building was raised at Sixth and Broadway in 1868, at a cost of about $145,000, the pews in the sanctuary were divided into five classes: 12 pews at $1,250 each, 32 at $1,000 each, 34 at $700 each, 76 at $450 each, and 56 at $250 each. For the third Adath Israel temple, nine classes of pews were designated. The most expensive class comprised six pews to be auctioned for a minimum of $3,000 each. The least expensive class, to be auctioned for a minimum of only $100 each, comprised eighteen pews on the main floor of the sanctuary and all fifty-six pews in the temple's balcony. The balcony seats were placed in the least expensive category, the subcommittee on seating explained, because "we have no experience with this location and do not know how our members take to it."[11]

While mass solicitation and the sale of seats was often what allowed a congregation to cover the cost of acquiring a building, sometimes the acquisition of a synagogue depended on the willingness of only a handful of concerned families or individuals to make large financial contributions. In Hopkinsville, for example, it was apparently a $5,000 bequest from Henry Bohn that started the community on its way toward constructing a synagogue; and in Lexington it was a $25,000 donation from Leo Marks in memory of his father, given with the understanding that the congregation would provide a matching amount, that enabled Adath Israel to construct a temple. In Ashland it seems that Joseph Mansbach and his four brothers-in-law were the ones who undertook the building of a synagogue for the town's Orthodox congregation just after World War II.[12]

In Kentucky's smaller Jewish communities, several congregations never did reach the point of acquiring buildings of their own. The first two congregations in Lexington both met in rented space during all the years of their existence. In the nineteenth century the Spinoza Society made frequent use of a hall at the corner of Short and Limestone Streets for its activities, and Brith Jacob—an Orthodox congregation organized just before World War I—met in an upper-story room at 351 West Short Street throughout its brief life span. Among all the Kentucky Jewish congregations that are now defunct, five never occupied homes of their own. The congregation that functioned longest without its own building was southeastern Kentucky's B'nai Sholom, although this assembly did achieve a certain sense of permanence by occupying the same rented hall in Harlan during the last quarter-century of its existence.[13]

Even though most of Kentucky's Jewish congregations had to function in temporary quarters for some years, and even though some were never able to acquire their own facilities, a few assemblies in the commonwealth were able to move into their own synagogue buildings very soon after they were founded. In late nineteenth-century Louisville, for example, Brith Sholom erected its first building just a year after the congregation was established, and Adath Jeshurun acquired its first synagogue, a converted church, in the same year the assembly was organized. In fact, it seems that in a few cases a group of like-minded worshipers formed a congregation precisely because they wanted to acquire a synagogue building in which to carry on their activities. In Lexington, it appears that both Adath Israel and Ohavay Zion were created so that permanent places of worship could be established, first for the Reform Jews in the city and, soon after, for its Orthodox residents.

Figure 8. Adath Israel, Maryland Avenue, Lexington. This church building served as the first home of Adath Israel, from 1905 until 1926, when the congregation erected a new temple.

The first Jewish families to arrive in Lexington were generally attracted to the liberalized practices of Reform Judaism, and it was they who organized the Spinoza Society soon after the Civil War. At the turn of the twentieth century, however, the Spinoza Society seems to have been languishing as a congregational body, and so the established Jews of Lexington, apparently set on revitalizing their congregational life and opening a temple, determined to create a new religious institution. Their Adath Israel congregation was officially chartered in 1904, and by 1905 it had acquired a former church to use as a permanent place of worship.[14] This structure was the first actual synagogue in Lexington (see Figure 8).

The more religiously observant Jews of Lexington, primarily East European immigrants, also put the purchase of a building high on their list of priorities when they founded Ohavay Zion in 1912. An often

Figure 9. Ohavay Zion, Maxwell Street, Lexington. Originally a Presbyterian church, this building served as a synagogue for most of the twentieth century, and was then transformed into a restaurant.

repeated oral tradition tells how the decision to establish this congregation was reached. It seems that in 1911 the Orthodox Jews of Lexington were conducting Yom Kippur services at the local Odd Fellows hall (perhaps under the auspices of the Brith Jacob congregation) when a number of lodge members burst in upon the proceedings, intending to hold their regular meeting. One version of the story relates that the lodge members had rented out their hall without realizing that Yom Kippur fell on the night they usually gathered there; another version maintains that the religious services were lasting longer than expected because a visiting rabbi had been invited to deliver an impromptu sermon. In any event, the worshipers found themselves out on the sidewalk without having concluded the liturgy, and it is said that they vowed then and there to create a new congregation and to secure a permanent place of worship. Within a year the new Ohavay Zion congre-

Figure 10. Congregants in front of the Keneseth Israel synagogue on Jacob Avenue in Louisville, at its dedication in 1929. From the University of Louisville Photographic Archives, Caufield and Shook Collection (neg. 104907).

gation had arranged to acquire a Presbyterian church on Maxwell Street to use as their synagogue, and they moved into the converted building in 1914 (see Figure 9).[15]

Another Kentucky congregation that seems to have been established with the question of a proper place of worship in mind was Louisville's Keneseth Israel, created in 1926 when B'nai Jacob and Beth Hamedrash Hagodol merged in an effort to overcome their financial difficulties and to deal with the inadequacies of their respective meetinghouses. For a few years the new congregation met in the Beth Hamedrash Hagodol synagogue, but merger made it possible for Keneseth Israel to launch an ambitious building campaign, and in 1929 the young congregation dedicated a brand new sanctuary at the corner of Jacob and Floyd Streets (see Figure 10).[16]

The second quarter of the twentieth century witnessed a marked decline in the number of new Jewish congregations being formed in

Kentucky, as the Bolshevik Revolution in Russia and the imposition of severe immigration restrictions in the United States slowed the arrival of Jewish immigrants from Eastern Europe to a trickle. As Table 2 indicates, only seven new congregations have appeared in Kentucky since 1931, all of them established since the end of World War II. Two of these were the short-lived Blue Grass Judean Society of Danville, which formed around a nucleus of doctors and patients from the local state hospital, and Temple Israel of Covington, which represented an ulti-mately unsuccessful attempt by a few new arrivals in northern Ken-tucky to revive Jewish communal life in that part of the state. During the short period of its existence, the Danville congregation held services above a store on Main Street. The Covington congregation of the late 1960s and early 1970s met in an auditorium at Thomas More College. The group looked into the possibility of rehabilitating the synagogue of the city's original Temple of Israel congregation, but it was unable to do so, and the assembly dissolved within a decade of its founding.[17]

Perhaps the most notable Kentucky congregation to be established since the end of World War II is The Temple in Louisville. This assembly was created in 1976 by the merger of two of the city's oldest congrega-tions, Adath Israel and Brith Sholom. The union of these two Reform congregations was motivated primarily by the desire of both groups to improve their physical facilities (parking was a major problem) and to relocate to the eastern part of Jefferson County, an area that was attracting an increasing number of Jewish residents. Indeed, Adath Israel had begun planning for a new building even before its merger with Brith Sholom. For a few years after it was organized, The Temple held services in the building Brith Sholom had erected in the 1950s (Figure 56), and in 1980 the congregation was able to move into an imposing new sanctuary on Brownsboro Road (Figure 64).[18]

Although it is clear that most of Louisville's Reform Jews approved of the merger of Adath Israel and Brith Sholom, there were still some in the community, especially among members of Brith Sholom, who wanted an alternative to the extremely large congregational body that resulted. It was these individuals who founded Temple Shalom.[19] Like many other new congregations in Kentucky over the years, Temple Shalom began its life in temporary quarters. It met first at the Jewish Community Center of Louisville and then in the chapel of Bellarmine College, a local Catholic institution. Not until 1981 was Temple Shalom able to purchase a private home and convert it for use as a place of worship (see Figures 11 and 12). It remained in that facility until 1989, when the congregation moved into its new sanctuary, Kentucky's most recently constructed synagogue building (Figure 59).

Over the last quarter-century or so, some American Jews have begun to express uneasiness over what they have perceived as the impersonality of large congregations with very formal worship services.

Figure 11. Temple Shalom, Taylorsville Road, Louisville. From 1981 to 1989, this private home served as the synagogue of the newly formed Temple Shalom congregation.

Figure 12. The lawn sign that marked the home of Louisville's Temple Shalom in the 1980s. It is now displayed in front of the congregation's sanctuary on Lowe Road.

This not only has prompted some established synagogues to modify certain of their practices, but has also led small groups within the American Jewish community to seek new forms of religious organization that foster a greater sense of warmth in prayer and closeness in social interaction. It has been suggested that the disappearance of extended families as support networks is also partly responsible for motivating some Jews to search for more intimate religious institutions.

One type of organizational structure that has been spawned by the search for new modes of religious expression is the *havurah* (literally, a "fellowship"). Designed specifically to allow their members to share prayer, study, and social interaction within a relaxed atmosphere, *havurot* (plural of *havurah*) generally hold their gatherings in individual homes or other informal settings, and they operate on the basis of lay participation, usually without employing a rabbi, cantor, or other salaried functionary. As its name implies, the Lexington Havurah has organized itself in accordance with the philosophy of the *havurah* movement, and it is one of only two Kentucky congregations operating today without its own house of worship.

The search for a less rigid institutional structure and for greater intimacy and participation in the prayer service has also brought about the revival of small prayer houses, often referred to by the Yiddish term *shtiblach*. These prayer houses, generally Orthodox in practice, were once ubiquitous in American cities with large Jewish immigrant populations; Louisville congregations such as B'nai Jacob and Anshei Sfard might have been considered *shtiblach* in their earliest years. The Beth Israel congregation organized in 1985 (not associated in any way with Louisville's original congregation of that name) is a sort of contemporary *shtible* (singular of *shtiblach*). It occupies a converted house not far from the Anshei Sfard synagogue and the Jewish Community Center of Louisville (see Figure 13).

The creation of Kentucky's newest congregation, Adat B'nai Yisrael, reflects yet other recent phenomena affecting the American Jewish experience, including the adoption of non-traditional forms of family life and the trend toward intermarriage between Jews and Gentiles. This small group has defined itself as a "Liberal Reform" body whose organizational structure draws on the ideas of the *havurah* movement, and it has launched a campaign of outreach to the unaffiliated and disaffected. The congregation presents itself as an alternative for individuals who might not feel comfortable in other Louisville congregations, perhaps because of their marital status, or their homosexual lifestyles, or their financial circumstances. Adat B'nai Yisrael has announced its openness to all Jews together with their "spouses or partners," and it has indicated that congregants would be expected to support the congregation only "according to their means."

Figure 13. Beth Israel, Almara Circle, Louisville. This private home was purchased for use by the Orthodox Beth Israel congregation in 1985.

Recent studies have shown that although some 90 percent of American Jews who wed before 1965 married other Jews, the majority who have married since 1985 have married non-Jews.[20] Taking note of this development, all of Kentucky's Reform temples now accept non-Jewish spouses as members of their congregations, and Adat B'nai Yisrael's publicity has specifically stressed that the congregation will welcome "Jews, Jews-by-Choice [that is, converts] and non-Jews." Indeed, Adat B'nai Yisrael has announced that it will not only accommodate couples that are already intermarried but "be available to all Jews for lifecycle events, including marriages, whether the intended spouse is Jewish or non-Jewish."[21]

It has now been more than a century and a half since Kentucky's first Jewish congregation was organized, and in the intervening years more than two dozen other congregations have been established in the commonwealth. Some have flourished and prospered; others have transformed their identities over time; and still others have withered and died. What is clear, however, is that throughout the last 150 years, organized Jewish life has been a vital element in the complex religious and ethnic makeup of Kentucky. Without question, the presence of Jewish congregations has brought a distinctive extra dimension to the experience of all the larger cities of the commonwealth, and some of its smaller ones as well.

Maintaining synagogue buildings as local centers of Jewish activity is one of the most visible ways in which Jewish congregations have had an impact on urban culture in Kentucky over the years. The synagogues established by various Jewish congregations are an important part of the commonwealth's architectural heritage, and they tell a great deal about the Jewish communities they served. For both these reasons, they are worthy of particular attention. And so, having briefly told the story of how the commonwealth's individual Jewish congregations came into being, we now turn to a consideration of Kentucky's synagogue buildings, past and present.

Chapter 2

Kentucky Synagogue Buildings

A STORY IS TOLD ABOUT a Jewish traveler who, finding himself far from home one Sabbath, decided to attend services at a local synagogue. In order to make the stranger feel welcome, the congregation honored him by inviting him to participate in the ritual of the reading of the Torah. As he waited his turn to go up to the reader's table, the man noticed that all those who were called to the Torah before him walked about halfway down the aisle of the synagogue, stooped low, then straightened themselves and proceeded to the front of the sanctuary. The visitor had never before seen this unusual practice but, out of courtesy, he too stooped low in the aisle when he was called up to the Torah.

After the service, the extremely curious out-of-towner inquired about the reason for the peculiar custom he had witnessed. None of the congregants seemed to have the answer; the practice of stooping was rooted in the history of the congregation, and it had never been questioned. Finally, however, one of the elders of the community came forward with the explanation no one had ever thought to seek before: "At one time our synagogue had a large chandelier that hung low over the aisle, and people had to bend down to get under it. The chandelier was removed many years ago," the elderly gentleman continued, "but the stooping has continued nonetheless!"

This story is, of course, apocryphal, but it does make the point that the history and character of a congregation are very often bound closely to the history and physical appearance of its buildings. Synagogues can be powerful symbols of permanence and continuity, and important events in a congregation's history are frequently associated with the edifice in which they take place. By contrast, congregations without their own buildings must feel a certain sense of transiency and instability.

The story of the synagogue where people continued to stoop even after their chandelier was removed also calls attention to the fact that a synagogue (or a temple, to use the term preferred in Reform circles) not only reflects the identity of the congregation that uses it but also has the power, in some respects, to condition a congregation's behavior and its very nature. The outward appearance of a synagogue, its interior configuration, the specific uses for which it is designed—all these manifest the thinking that went into planning the building and affect the outlook and the actions of those who make use of it. In a sense, the physical environment of a synagogue is like the text of a synagogue liturgy, which (as scholars concerned with issues of gender have emphasized in recent years) both reflects the conditions under which it was composed and influences the perceptions of those who recite it. This is why knowing about a congregation's synagogue can reveal so much about the way its members view themselves and about the way they conduct their various activities.

The physical arrangement of a synagogue's worship space, for example, can tell a lot about the nature of the religious rites that are conducted within the sanctuary and about the way members of the congregation interact with each other and with their clergy. The floor plans of traditional synagogues in America, borrowing from European models, have always been determined primarily by the placement of the two key features of every synagogue interior: the ark containing the sacred Torah scrolls, and the reader's platform, or *bimah*, where the Torah is read and from which the cantor or prayer leader generally conducts services.

In traditional synagogues in Europe and America, the ark has usually been placed on the eastern wall of the sanctuary, so that the axis of the worship space is oriented toward the holy city of Jerusalem. In most cases, the ark has been positioned somewhat higher than floor level, with steps and a rostrum before it. The *bimah* has generally been placed near the center of the worship space in such a way that the Torah reader or prayer leader faces the ark. A lectern facing the congregation would be used in a traditional synagogue only for sermons (relatively recent innovations in Judaism) or for other proceedings not inherently a part of the worship service.

The centrally placed *bimah* of the traditional synagogue plan has usually been accompanied by seating arranged along three sides of a square or perhaps in a curved pattern around the platform. Sometimes seats facing the front of the sanctuary have been placed in the space between the *bimah* and the ark, and often the square or circle of seating is completed by providing chairs for a few individuals (perhaps the rabbi or the congregational elders) on the rostrum along the ark wall.

In a variation on the traditional synagogue arrangement which has become increasingly common in the twentieth century, the reader's platform is moved to the front of the sanctuary and merged with the rostrum before the ark. The reader's table still faces the ark, however, and is sometimes placed somewhat lower than the platform immediately before the ark. In this layout the entire raised area at the front of the hall is usually referred to as the *bimah*.

The traditional synagogue arrangement, especially if it retains a central *bimah*, avoids creating a single fixed focus of attention within the sanctuary; there are at least two, the ark and the reader's platform. A central *bimah* also fosters a certain sense of contact among worshipers by having them face inward rather than forward. All this tends to create a feeling of intimacy and common participation in the worship experience, allowing those present to drift freely between intense involvement with the prayer service and social interaction with one another. In addition, the traditional *bimah* placement emphasizes the role of the cantor or reader as a representative of the congregation, rather than as a member of a privileged hierarchy separate from the body of worshipers. And because the traditional arrangement of the synagogue space does not enforce concentration on a single spot or person, it acknowledges the traditional Jewish belief that prayer, though conducted in a communal setting, is essentially an inwardly directed, personal experience.[1]

Over the years, however, many American synagogues—in Kentucky as elsewhere—have abandoned the traditional floor plan based on a forward-facing reader's platform positioned either at the center or toward the front of the worship space. Instead, they have transformed the *bimah* into a sort of stage by turning the main reader's table toward the congregation and creating a seating configuration much like that of an auditorium. Sometimes the reader's table is shifted to one side of the *bimah* and balanced by a second lectern on the other side. Room may also be provided at the front of the hall for a choir and (in Reform temples) for an organ.

Influenced to some extent by the model of Protestant churches, this newer layout of the synagogue interior was designed in part to make more efficient use of seating space in the hall, but it was also intended to focus more attention on the rabbi and cantor and thus to introduce an atmosphere of greater refinement into synagogue services. In traditional synagogues there was little concern with prayer in unison, and so the proceedings generally lacked the decorum that characterized the church services of most mainstream Christian denominations. Taking into account the norms of American society at large, many congregations saw the lack of gentility in traditional services as problematic, and they hoped that adoption of the new synagogue arrangement would introduce greater decorum into Jewish worship. The auditorium arrangement in synagogues was widely adopted in Reform congregations in the nineteenth century; in some temples the choir was made a center of attention along with the clergy, although in others the organ and singers were hidden behind the ark or at the rear of the hall in an effort to enhance the otherworldly mood of the sanctuary. By the twentieth century, the new synagogue design began to spread more widely, reflecting important changes in the way American Jews, including those in Kentucky, have behaved at prayer.

Synagogue seating arrangements have also been influenced by changing attitudes toward women's roles in the worship service. Because of their familial obligations in traditional society, the *halacha*, the Jewish legal code, has exempted women from most timebound ritual obligations, including public worship. This has meant that in Orthodox circles women have been seen as marginal in the public worship experience. Additionally, Jewish tradition has viewed the intimate presence of women as a distraction for men engaged in prayer, which is considered an obligatory activity for them. Seating arrangements in traditional synagogues have for centuries reflected these views, and so women have invariably been assigned to peripheral seating in houses of worship designed in accordance with *halacha*. They have been relegated either to galleries above the space reserved for men or, in more recent times, to separate areas behind or at the side of the main worship space.

Neither Reform Judaism nor Conservative Judaism has retained the practice of separate seating by gender, however. Reform Judaism, less bound to tradition than other branches of the faith and more concerned with adapting Jewish worship to American norms, adopted mixed seating and family pews quite early in its development. If Reform temples were built with balconies, the galleries were intended to increase seating capacity, rather than to create a separate space for women. Conservative Judaism gave up gender-segregated seating more slowly, but with its rather flexible approach to *halacha* it too sanctioned mixed seating as it moved toward accepting the idea of equal status for women and men in the context of public worship. The more recently developed branch of Judaism labeled Traditional also tends to favor mixed seating, although it still resists the idea of allowing women to conduct synagogue services when men are present. All this has of course caused fundamental alterations in the way synagogue interiors have been designed over the years; consequently, a congregation's ideology can often be read in the floor plan of its sanctuary. As the historian Jonathan Sarna has written concerning the debate over mixed seating in American synagogues, "Where people sit reveals much about what they believe."[2]

Even something as seemingly mundane as a decision about what kind of seats to install in a synagogue sanctuary can be a revealing indicator of the assumptions made by the designers of the hall and an important factor in determining what will go on within it. The point can perhaps best be made with reference to two Louisville synagogues built in the quarter-century after World War II, those of Adath Jeshurun and Keneseth Israel.

At Adath Jeshurun, upholstered fold-down auditorium seats were installed, the rows rather close together and with no place provided for book storage. The assumption of those who arranged this seating seems to have been that persons attending services would remain in their places, holding their prayer books and Bibles, throughout the entire liturgy. The environment they created has, in fact, made it difficult for worshipers to move around the worship space freely or to engage in the kind of rhythmic swaying that has often accompanied traditional Jewish prayer. Moreover, the seating arrangement in the sanctuary makes it difficult for parents to bring young children to services, and at least for a time the synagogue had a reputation for discouraging the presence of youngsters. The congregation now makes babysitting available on the Sabbath and holidays, and it also has a Junior Congregation program, but, of course, these services only indirectly address the inhospitableness of the main sanctuary to children. As a congregation, Adath Jeshurun now in fact welcomes family participation, but to some extent it has become the victim of its own seating arrangement.

By contrast, the seating at Keneseth Israel is in pews with plenty of space between them and convenient racks for book storage. The aisles at Keneseth Israel are wide, and there is a large open space at the back of the sanctuary. All this creates a sense of spaciousness and relative informality in the hall. It is fairly easy to enter and leave the pews; there is room to sway; and children can be present without being confined to narrow seats in which they would tend to become restless. Keneseth Israel's seating arrangement reflects an understanding of the need for room to move about in a traditional synagogue sanctuary, and it both accommodates traditional behavior in prayer and encourages the presence of children.

If the interiors of synagogues can reveal a lot about the congregations they serve, so too can the exteriors of these buildings. The outward appearance of a synagogue says a great deal about the self-image of the congregational community that inhabits it and about the way that community wishes to represent itself to the general public. On the one hand, congregations that built imposing structures on major thoroughfares were likely to be saying something not only about the impressive size of their assemblies and the material success of their members but also about their desire to be recognized as essential elements in their urban communities. On the other hand, congregations that erected more humble structures or moved into existing buildings were revealing something about the more modest circumstances of their members and perhaps also about their lesser degree of concern with public recognition. It is not by chance that the grandest and most conspicuously sited of Kentucky's synagogues—the Adath Israel buildings on Broadway and on Third Street in Louisville, for example, or the Temple Israel building on Broadway in Paducah (Figures 21, 35, and 31)—have been those erected by Reform congregations, reflecting both the relative affluence of Reform Jews in Kentucky and their greater concern with demonstrating that they are in the mainstream of American life.

It is because the histories of individual congregations are so closely associated with their buildings, and because these buildings reveal so much about those who built and used them, that preserving information about Kentucky's synagogues is such an important task. With this in mind, Table 4, page 153, summarizes basic information about every site where a synagogue is known to have stood in Kentucky from the time the state's first Jewish house of worship was erected in 1849 until the present. The table lists synagogue sites in order of the date they were occupied and provides information about their exact locations and also about which congregations were located there.

Of course, Table 4 does not list every locale where Jewish worship services have been conducted in the commonwealth. As we have seen, Jews have gathered to pray in a wide variety of settings over the years. The Livingston store in Paducah, the Kentucky Bakery building in Henderson, and the Odd Fellows halls of Louisville, Covington, and Lexington were all places where Jewish worship services were held at one time or another, but they cannot properly be considered synagogues and, consequently, are not represented in the table. More specifically, private homes or shops where Jewish worship might have taken place from time to time and rented spaces in buildings that were generally used for purposes other than holding religious services have been excluded from the inventory—as have Jewish chapels installed in buildings that have not themselves been the homes of Jewish congregations. This means, for example, that the chapel maintained since 1949 at Four Courts, the Louisville Jewish community's home for the elderly, is not listed; neither are the chapels located in the buildings that have housed Eliahu Academy, the Louisville Jewish Day School. The sites included in Table 4 are only those of buildings that served *primarily* as Jewish places of worship at one time or another in their history.

In most cases, only a single Jewish congregation has occupied each of the sites listed, but three synagogue buildings in Louisville have served first one congregation and later another. The first was the synagogue built by the Brith Sholom congregation and later sold to Anshei Sfard. The other two passed from old congregations to newly created ones as the result of mergers: when Beth Hamedrash Hagodol joined with B'nai Jacob to create Keneseth Israel, the newly formed congregation moved into the Beth Hamedrash Hagodol synagogue for a time; when Brith Sholom merged with Adath Israel to form The Temple, that new congregation made use of the Brith Sholom building for several years.

The street number given for each site in Table 4 is generally the one in use at the end of the period when the property in question served as the location of a synagogue. Thus, the First Street synagogue that served as a place of worship for Brith Sholom and later for Anshei Sfard is listed as being at 509 South First Street, even though its address was 613 First Street before the Louisville street numbering system was altered early in the twentieth century, and even though at various times it was also listed as being at 523 and 513 South First Street. Similarly, the address given for B'nai Jacob's property is 432 East Jefferson, even though over the years it was also given as 456, 454, and 430 East Jefferson.

From time to time in various Kentucky cities, not only numbering systems but street names have changed. In Louisville, for example, a portion of Green Street was for a time named Fehr Avenue, and now the entire street is called Liberty. In Paducah the nineteenth century's Chestnut Street is now South Fifth Street. In those few cases where a synagogue stood on a street whose name was subsequently changed, Table 4 retains the street name in use at the time of the synagogue's existence.

The date of initial occupancy given for each of the synagogue sites listed in Table 4 is the date when a Jewish congregation began using the location as its principal meeting place, rather than when the congregation acquired the site. In several cases where a congregation built a new synagogue on property it had purchased, construction began in one year but was not completed until the next. Thus in a few instances the year inscribed on a synagogue's cornerstone does not coincide with the year of initial occupancy given in Table 4. The cornerstone of Henderson's Adas Israel (Figure 14) bears the date 1891, for example, but the

Figure 14. The cornerstone of Adas Israel, Henderson. The date indicates that construction of the building was begun the year before it was occupied.

building was not completed until 1892; and the cornerstone of Adath Israel's Third Street building in Louisville reads 1905, although the congregation did not leave its Broadway temple and relocate to its new sanctuary until 1906. Similarly, although the cornerstone of Covington's first Temple of Israel is inscribed 1915 (Figure 1), the building was not occupied until 1916; and although the cornerstone of the second Temple of Israel reads 1938, that building was not dedicated until 1939. Most of the cornerstones of Kentucky's synagogues, incidentally, are engraved not only with a secular date but also with the Jewish calendar year written in Hebrew characters.

It should also be noted that some congregations settled into their new homes only gradually. Recall, for example, that Beth Hamedrash Hagodol apparently conducted its activities in a dwelling on the grounds of the German Lutheran Church it had bought while the church itself was being renovated for use as a synagogue. Thus, even though the date of occupancy for the Beth Hamedrash Hagodol property on Preston Street is given in Table 4 as 1905, the congregation did not begin using the main building at that site until at least two years later.

Two Louisville congregations first made use of existing structures at their synagogue sites and only later erected their own houses of worship there. B'nai Jacob acquired a former church to use as its home in 1891, but it demolished that structure at the turn of the century and erected a new synagogue building in its place. Similarly, in 1950 the Brith Sholom congregation sold its downtown temple and moved all its operations to an existing building on the school grounds it had purchased two years earlier in the Highlands neighborhood (see Figure 15). That building, often referred to as the Bonnycastle Mansion, was dubbed Brith Sholom's "Temple House" in 1949. Only in 1951, however, did the congregation dedicate the first part of a new temple building on its Highlands property, and it did not complete the construction of its main sanctuary there until 1956 (see Figure 56).

Adath Jeshurun handled its move to the Highlands somewhat differently. Almost immediately after it bought the Woodbourne Avenue estate of Eleanor Beard in 1951, the congregation began using the twelve-room residence on that property for some of its activities; this building was referred to as the congregation's "Community House" for several years. Unlike Brith Sholom, however, Adath Jeshurun did not sell its downtown synagogue and move its principal operations to the Highlands until its new house of worship was completed in 1957.[3]

Other examples of what might be called a gradual settling-in come from the histories of two other Louisville congregations, Anshei Sfard and Keneseth Israel. Both congregations dedicated their new suburban synagogue facilities well before their main assembly halls were constructed: the sanctuary of the 1958 Anshei Sfard complex was added only in 1963, and that of the 1964 Keneseth Israel building was added

Figure 15. The Bonnycastle estate on Cowling Avenue in Louisville, which the Brith Sholom congregation acquired in 1948. The main building on the site, being used as a private school when this photograph was taken in 1928, later became Brith Sholom's classroom building. From the University of Louisville Photographic Archives, Caufield and Shook Collection (neg. 95753).

only in 1971. As a consequence, the Anshei Sfard building has two cornerstones, while the sole cornerstone of the Keneseth Israel synagogue (Figure 16) is misleadingly dated 1971.

Although it was rather unusual for a congregation to move to a new site and only then to begin renovating or building its main sanctuary, it was not unusual for a congregation to continue to add to its facilities over the years. Many of Kentucky's synagogue buildings underwent significant alterations during the time they served their congregations. In 1898, for example, a school building was erected adjoining the Adath Israel sanctuary, which had stood at Sixth and Broadway since 1868. Similarly, in 1925 an auditorium building was annexed to the 1919 Adath Jeshurun synagogue. In Lexington the Adath Israel temple of

Figure 16. The cornerstone of the Keneseth Israel synagogue on Taylorsville Road in Louisville. This stone shows the date when the main sanctuary was erected, rather than the date when the original building was constructed.

Figure 17. Adath Israel on Ashland Avenue in Lexington. This aerial photograph, taken around 1986, shows the original 1926 temple and its more recent expansion. Photograph courtesy of the Central Kentucky Jewish Federation, Lexington.

1926 was expanded in 1950 and again in 1955 with the addition of religious school facilities. In 1984 the temple underwent another major renovation and expansion (see Figure 17). New wings were also added over the years to the Ohavay Zion synagogue on Maxwell Street: a social hall was dedicated in 1941, and a school wing in 1964. At the 1957 Adath Jeshurun building in Louisville a classroom extension was dedicated in 1966 (Figure 71), and at the 1964 Keneseth Israel synagogue an additional auditorium wing was added in 1982.

Perhaps no Kentucky synagogue changed its basic appearance more dramatically than did the First Street synagogue erected by Louisville's Brith Sholom congregation in 1881. This structure was originally designed as a long rectangular meetinghouse, and it underwent only minor refurbishing at the time Anshei Sfard acquired the building at the turn of the century. In 1928, however, Anshei Sfard added a two-story annex that contained a social hall on the second floor and seating space for women on the first (Anshei Sfard was an Orthodox congregation that maintained gender-segregated seating). An imposing new facade, erected to tie the old and new units of the synagogue together, gave the First Street synagogue an appearance completely different from the look it had during the first half-century of its existence (compare Figures 22 and 43).

Of all the synagogue buildings in Kentucky, only fifteen were erected as Jewish places of worship and never served any other purpose;

these include the nine synagogues that are still in use by Jewish congregations today. All the other synagogues in the state were either buildings converted from a previous use, or buildings eventually given over to a subsequent use, or buildings that had a history both before and after they served as synagogues. Table 5 presents a summary of the life course of each of Kentucky's synagogue buildings. Like the synagogue sites in Table 4, the buildings in Table 5 are listed by their date of occupancy as synagogues. For each building that was not constructed as a synagogue, the table indicates the former function that the structure served; for each building that fulfilled some other purpose after it ceased to be a synagogue, the table indicates its subsequent function. Table 5 also identifies which of the commonwealth's synagogue buildings are still standing and provides the date of demolition for those that have disappeared from the landscape.

It should be noted that Table 5 indicates only the immediate former and subsequent uses of those synagogue buildings that served other functions. A few synagogue buildings in the commonwealth, however, passed through more than just two or three hands during their lifetimes. The B'nai Jacob building of 1891 (Figure 24) was the African American community's Plymouth Congregational Church just before it became a synagogue, for example, but earlier in the 1880s it had been a Baptist church. As already noted, B'nai Jacob erected a new synagogue on the site of its converted church in 1901 (Figure 34). When that structure was sold by the congregation, it became the Italian American Club, and still later it served as the St. Michael Orthodox Church. The impressive building that Louisville's Brith Sholom acquired in 1903 (Figure 26) had been built as a Presbyterian church, but before Brith Sholom moved in it had stood vacant for two years and then had served for a short time as the home of a Baptist congregation.

When Beth Israel disbanded in 1894, its synagogue in downtown Louisville (Figure 19) became the home of an African American congregation, the Central Baptist Church, but by 1898 the building had been turned into a mission, and by 1900 it had become an industrial establishment. For a few years it served as a planing mill, and for several years after 1905 it was the workshop of the Louisville Organ and Orchestrion Company. The building was apparently torn down around 1911, and in its place a stable was erected to serve the Cuscaden Ice Cream Works.

Because so many of Kentucky's Jewish congregations had their beginnings in the nineteenth century or very early in the twentieth, several have occupied two or even three different sites during the course of their existence. Like a congregation's acquisition of its first building, each of its relocations was a significant milestone, often marking congregational growth and frequently reflecting changing residential patterns. In order to track the migrations of individual Kentucky Jewish congregations that moved from one synagogue site to another, Table 6, organized alphabetically by congregational name, identifies all the synagogue sites that each assembly occupied throughout its history. It also indicates which of Kentucky's Jewish congregations never had a synagogue building of its own.

Just as tracing the histories of Kentucky's various Jewish congregations can reveal a lot about the changing geography of Jewish life around the commonwealth, so tracking various congregations as they moved from one location to another within the same city can help us gauge changing patterns of Jewish settlement in a given urban area. In Louisville, where the migration of Jewish congregations within the city is most apparent, changing synagogue locations clearly reveal how the geographic center of Jewish life has shifted over the last century and a half.

The sites of Louisville's first two synagogues indicate that the initial center of Jewish life in the city was in the middle of the downtown area; both the original Adath Israel building and the Beth Israel synagogue were within a block and a half of what is now the corner of Third Street and Liberty. The location of the city's synagogues at the end of the century, however, suggests that the hub of the Jewish community had by then shifted eastward. A hundred years ago, three of Louisville's four synagogues could be found within a limited area bounded by Jefferson Street to the north, Chestnut Street to the south, Jackson Street to the east, and Second Street to the west. Only the imposing Reform temple of Adath Israel at Broadway and Sixth was outside the main area of Jewish concentration at the time (see Map 4).

Like other American Jewish communities whose populations were burgeoning in the era of East European immigration, Louisville's Jewish community was becoming clearly subdivided as the end of the nineteenth century approached. A quite distinct separation was apparent between the city's long-established families and the community's more recently arrived, usually less prosperous families. The former were primarily of central European origin and tended to identify with Reform Judaism. The latter were generally of East European origin and, if they were at all religiously inclined, tended to identify with a more traditional outlook. One descendant of a member of Adath Israel, Louisville's first and most militantly Reform congregation, relates that in the early twentieth century, members of the temple would go so far as to cross the street in order to avoid an encounter with someone from a more traditional congregation.

The spatial separation of the Adath Israel temple from the city's other synagogues at the end of the nineteenth century suggests that the social subdivision within the city's Jewish community had a geographic component as well, and this geographic subdivision can be detected even more clearly in the pattern of synagogue location on the eve of

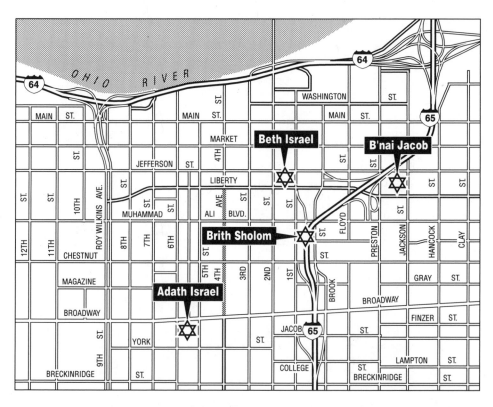

Map 4. Downtown Louisville in the early 1990s, showing location of synagogue buildings in 1892.

World War I. At that time, the four synagogues serving the more religiously observant elements of Louisville Jewry were all in the well-established Jewish neighborhood just north of Broadway between Second Street and Jackson (the synagogues here were often referred to as *shuls*, from the Yiddish word for school, reflecting the fact that in traditional society synagogues were also the places where men met to study). On the other hand, the two temples serving Louisville's more liberal congregations were now located south of Broadway (see Map 5). This indicates rather clearly that the more religiously traditional Jews of Louisville, primarily immigrants and their children, were concentrated in an organic neighborhood north of Broadway, while the more acculturated and assimilated element of the city's Jewish community was to be found farther uptown. It is perhaps symbolic that the Orthodox Anshei Sfard congregation took over the synagogue of Brith Sholom, when that liberal congregation moved farther south (Brith Sholom, sometimes labeled Conservative in its early decades, officially joined the Reform movement in 1920). The Conservative Adath Jeshurun congregation and the Orthodox Keneseth Israel built their synagogues south of Broadway only after World War I (see Map 6).

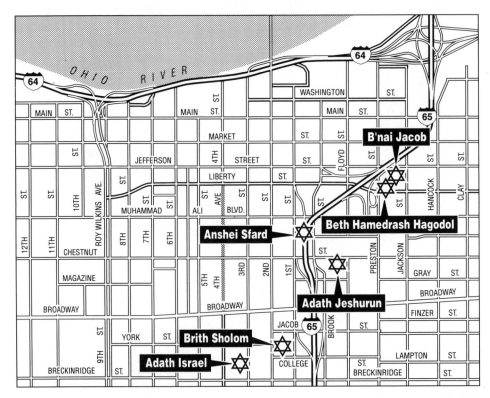

Map 5. Downtown Louisville in the early 1990s, showing location of synagogue buildings in 1912.

The wholesale relocation of Louisville's synagogues in the two decades after World War II signals yet another geographic shift of the local Jewish population: the migration of great numbers of Jewish families to the Highlands neighborhood as the city expanded and as all elements of its Jewish population became more affluent. The movement of Jews out of downtown and into the Highlands began in earnest in the 1920s and culminated in the years just after the Second World War. So dramatic was this movement that when a short history of Brith Sholom was prepared early in the 1950s, it already referred to the Highlands as "the center of the Jewish population" in Louisville. When the leaders of Adath Jeshurun unveiled the plans for their congregation's new sanctuary in the Highlands in 1955, they were able to declare that the building was going up "near the homes of 88 per cent of our members."[4]

The migration of Louisville Jews to the Highlands in the postwar era, like many earlier developments within the community, mirrored a nationwide trend. In just about every American city with a substantial Jewish population, a move toward the suburbs was under way by the time World War II broke out. Within a couple of decades, older areas of Jewish settlement in many downtown areas all over the country were

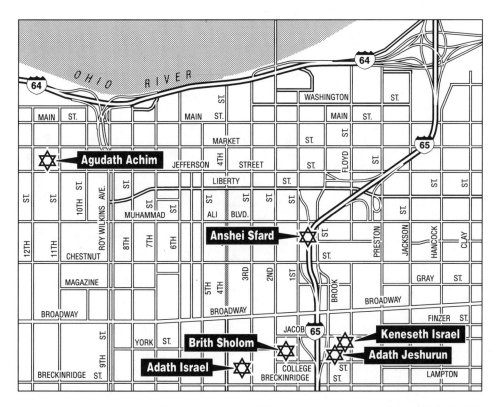

Map 6. Downtown Louisville in the early 1990s, showing location of synagogue buildings in 1930.

completely abandoned. The Reform Brith Sholom congregation was the first in Louisville to move out to the Highlands, and by 1965, four of the city's five congregations had become established there (see Map 7). As Table 5 indicates, five of the downtown buildings that had once been Louisville synagogues were torn down in the 1960s.

The migration of Jews out of city centers and their reconcentration in new suburban neighborhoods was not the last major change in American Jewish settlement patterns. During the 1970s yet another population shift was becoming apparent in many of the country's urban areas. As American Jews became increasingly unconcerned with traditional religious practice, many of them found geographic concentration irrelevant. Individuals who did not consider themselves governed by Jewish law saw no need to live near a kosher butcher shop, for example, or to reside within walking distance of their synagogue. Nor did they feel a need for the heavily ethnic cultural environment that had been so important to the Yiddish-speaking early generations of East European Jews in America.

By the later decades of the twentieth century, most American Jews were unwilling to forgo living in the attractive new subdivisions spring-

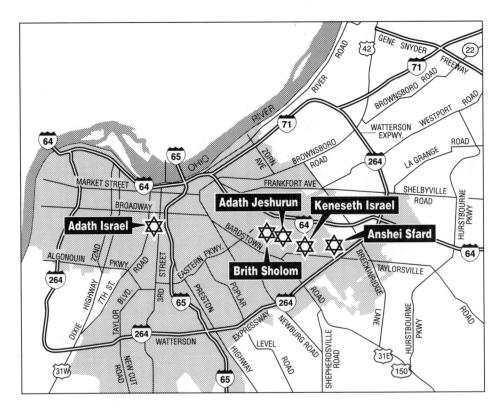

Map 7. Greater Louisville in the early 1990s, showing location of synagogue buildings in 1965.

ing up on the outskirts of many urban areas just so they could make their homes in Jewish neighborhoods. Moreover, they realized that new expressway systems and the proliferation of multi-car households provided a high degree of intraurban mobility for their families. Today, organic Jewish communities in which a great many families still live by a Jewish calendar and conduct their lives in accordance with *halacha* can be found only in America's largest cities. In Louisville, by 1991, only 20 percent of the city's Jews lived in the 40205 postal zone which includes the Highlands area; six other zip code zones were each home to 5 percent or more of the city's Jews; and no more than 1 percent of Louisville's Jews resided in the 40202 postal zone, the original area of Jewish settlement downtown.[5]

As large numbers of Jews began to move out of older suburbs and into widespread newer ones, their synagogues began to move farther out of the city as well. As in the past, Reform congregations tended to lead the way. Even though their members were now as likely to be the descendants of East European immigrants as of German-Jewish stock, these congregations were still likely to be more affluent than traditional congregations, and they were also less ideologically committed to Jew-

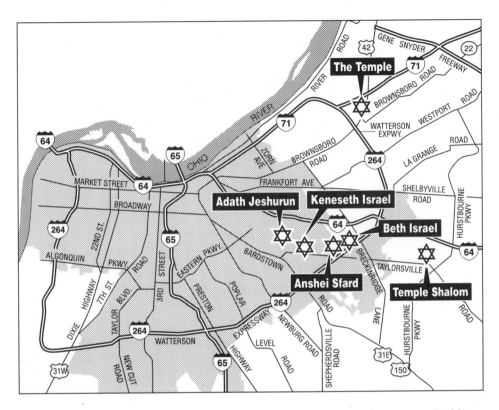

Map 8. Greater Louisville in the early 1990s, showing location of synagogue buildings in 1992.

ish distinctiveness and geographic cohesion. The most recent settlement trends among the Jews in Louisville, as well as the newest patterns of synagogue relocation, are reflected in the siting of the city's two Reform synagogues. Both The Temple on Brownsboro Road, erected in 1980 after the merger of Adath Israel and Brith Sholom, and Temple Shalom, constructed in 1989 on Lowe Road near Jeffersontown, Kentucky, stand in Louisville's newer eastern suburbs beyond the Watterson Expressway, the city's major beltway (see Map 8). And so, as the end of the twentieth century approaches, the pattern of synagogue location in Louisville reflects both the midcentury move of Jews to the Highlands and their more recent migration farther out into newer suburbs. In Lexington the recent relocation of the Ohavay Zion congregation to Edgewater Court also reflects the tendency of Jews to migrate away from the city center, in this case to the town's southeastern suburbs.

As we have already suggested, the architectural plan and the style of a congregation's synagogue have the ability both to disclose and to define the functions that take place within it. A synagogue can also mirror and influence congregational identity. The next two chapters examine the design and appearance of Kentucky's Jewish houses of worship in greater detail. Paying special attention to those structures built as synagogues rather than converted from other uses, these chapters explore the way in which synagogue architecture in Kentucky has changed over time and how it has reflected developments in American synagogue design more generally.

Chapter 3

The First Century of Synagogue Design

WHENEVER A JEWISH CONGREGATION in Kentucky undertook the construction of a new synagogue building, whether a century ago or only in the last decade, it had to face several fundamental questions. Where would the structure stand? What facilities would it house? How would it look? In arriving at answers to these and similar questions, Kentucky's Jewish congregations, like Jewish congregations elsewhere in the United States, had a great deal of liberty. Throughout America (and increasingly in Western Europe as well by the nineteenth century), governments generally refrained from imposing discriminatory restrictions on the construction of Jewish places of worship, as so many countries had done in the past. For the most part, congregations had the freedom to proceed with building plans as they wished.

As it happens, Kentucky Jews have not used their freedom of architectural expression to erect any synagogues that could be considered particularly innovative in design, but they have built their houses of worship in a wide variety of styles. Kentucky Jews have tended to follow national trends in synagogue construction, and as a result the history of synagogue design in the commonwealth reflects quite reliably the history of synagogue architecture in America as a whole. This is one of the things that makes a study of Kentucky synagogues so engaging and so instructive. Moreover, in order to gain a true sense of the state of synagogue design in America, we must consider how national trends were manifested at the local level, and we must take notice of the mundane as well as the extraordinary.

Throughout the last two hundred years, the central problem of synagogue architecture in the free societies of Europe and America has been how to construct buildings that would be recognizable to the public as places of worship but at the same time identifiable as distinctively Jewish institutions. Historically, one very common solution to this prob-

lem (perhaps reflecting Western Jewry's inclination toward accultura-
tion) has been to construct synagogue buildings whose outward appearance was very similar to that of the churches that Western Jews found
in their architectural environments. Of course, the ornamentation of
these synagogues remained Jewish in character, and their interiors
were often arranged quite differently from the interiors of churches,
especially if they were serving Orthodox congregations.

The common practice of mimicking Christian forms in synagogue
design has not gone uncriticized over the decades. After all, in struggling with the question of how a Jewish house of prayer should look, the
emancipated Jewish communities of Europe and America were engaged
in creating a new image of themselves vis-à-vis their Gentile neighbors.
Perhaps even more important, they were engaged in fashioning their
own self-image as well.

Concerned with the state of American synagogue design as early as
the era of World War I, the American Jewish architect Albert S. Gottlieb
urged those building meetinghouses for Jewish congregations to "express freely and naturally . . . the spirit of our religion instead of
servilely copying the outward expression of other creeds with which we
have nothing in common." He challenged architects to design synagogues and temples that "represent as nearly as possible what . . . are
the chief characteristics of the Jewish faith; solemnity, dignity, gran-
deur, nobility, and withal simplicity and clarity." In order to achieve
some uniformity and recognizability in synagogue design, Gottlieb
maintained that, just as Christians often placed crosses on their
churches, Jews should consistently adorn the exteriors of their houses of
worship with "the Tablets of the Law representing the contribution of
Moses and the Jews to the advancement of the world."[1]

In much the same vein, the social critic and cultural historian
Lewis Mumford lamented in 1925 that "far from externalizing the
Jewish spirit, the [synagogue] architect too often politely conceals it—as
though its exposure were bad form. Sometimes this is due to his own
uncertainty and weakness," Mumford continued, but "very often, no
doubt, it reflects the characteristics of the congregation, or of its dominant members."[2]

Despite such criticisms, contemporary church design, and public
architectural style more generally, have always retained some influence
on American synagogue design. The influence of contemporary architecture was already quite apparent in the construction of American synagogues in the colonial and early national periods. The Touro Synagogue
in Newport, Rhode Island, built in 1763 and now the oldest surviving
synagogue building in the United States, provides a case in point. The
exterior of this building exhibits features that mark it as a typical
Georgian structure: it has a rigid symmetry, a hipped roof, sash windows, and a small Palladian entry portico. Similarly, the Beth Elohim

Figure 18. Adath Israel, Fourth Street, Louisville. The image indicated by the arrow is the only known representation of Kentucky's first synagogue, which was built in 1849 and burned in 1866. From J.T. Palmatary's 1855 bird's-eye-view map of Louisville, in the boardroom of the Liberty National Bank, Louisville. Photo by Tom Fougerousse.

synagogue of 1794 in Charleston, South Carolina, was built with the kind of basilican floor plan and tall steeple common to many church buildings in the South in the Georgian period.

As a series of newly revived historical styles began to dominate church architecture in the second quarter of the nineteenth century, synagogue architecture was not far behind. One of the earliest revival styles to be adopted by designers of American synagogues was neoclassicism; when Charleston's Beth Elohim burned down in 1838, for example, it was replaced with a synagogue in the form of a Greek temple. But soon various medieval revival styles became popular as well. By the second half of the nineteenth century, synagogues were being built in Italianate and Romanesque styles, with their characteristic rounded arches, and in the Gothic mode, with pointed arches, ornate finials, corner towers, and rose windows.

In Kentucky only two synagogues were built before the outbreak of the Civil War, both in Louisville: the Adath Israel building erected in 1849, and the Beth Israel synagogue put up eight years later. The surviving pictorial images of the exteriors of the Adath Israel and Beth Israel synagogues suggest that they were both relatively unpretentious buildings that blended well with their surroundings (Figures 18 and 19). An 1852 review of Louisville's early history notes that while the

Figure 19. Beth Israel, Green Street, Louisville. This building of Italianate design was the second synagogue erected in Kentucky. It served its Orthodox congregation from 1857 until 1894. From *Louisville Illustrated* (Louisville, 1889); print courtesy of Samuel W. Thomas.

imposing Walnut Street Baptist Church had a value of $80,000 at midcentury, and the city's Catholic Cathedral had a value of $125,000, the value of the Adath Israel synagogue at the time was only $11,000. This is not to say that Kentucky's oldest synagogues were completely inconspicuous, however. Both these synagogues stood near the center of the city, and the same 1852 history that compared the monetary value of the various houses of worship in Louisville opined that despite its relatively low cost, the Adath Israel synagogue was "the most elegant [ecclesiastical] building in the city."[3] When Rabbi Isaac Leeser, one of the most important leaders of nineteenth-century American Judaism, visited Louisville in 1851, he too had praised the Adath Israel building. Although he lamented that the construction work "had not been well done and will require repairs before long," Leeser nonetheless lauded the structure as "a beautiful building having a pretty portico and a convenient arrangement within."[4]

The Beth Israel synagogue as well had a certain presence. It was a substantial building whose design reflected some of the latest developments in urban architecture; its facade was dominated by a central entry door and three second-story windows, all with rounded arches and hood moldings of the type that characterized the newly popular Italianate style. Indeed, the Beth Israel building of 1857 bears a striking resemblance to the Christian Church erected only a few years later at Chestnut and Floyd, a building which was destined to become the first home of congregation Adath Jeshurun (compare Figures 19 and 25).

We have very little information about the interiors of either of Louisville's first Jewish sanctuaries, but from the travel memoir of Rabbi Leeser we know that the Adath Israel building was designed in such a way that its seating capacity could be expanded and, although Adath Israel subsequently adopted Reform practice, that its first synagogue had a separate women's gallery. We can assume that Beth Israel too had separate seating for men and women and, judging from the arrangement of windows revealed in the lone surviving photograph of this building, it appears to have been designed with a women's gallery extending around three sides of the synagogue interior.

As Table 5 indicates, neither the Adath Israel building of 1849 nor the Beth Israel synagogue of 1857 was still serving Louisville's Jewish community at the end of the nineteenth century. The Adath Israel building burned down in a spectacular fire in 1866 (excerpts from a newspaper account of this fire appear as Appendix A), and the Beth Israel building was vacated in 1894 when the congregation disbanded.

Aside from the two pre-Civil War synagogues in Louisville, which had been either destroyed or vacated by 1900, there was only one other synagogue building erected in Kentucky during the nineteenth century that did not survive into the twentieth. This was the original Bene Yeshurum synagogue in Paducah, built in 1871. This structure seems to have been a far less stately edifice than either of its Louisville predecessors. The Jewish distilling magnate and philanthropist Isaac Wolfe Bernheim, who lived in Paducah at the time its first synagogue was dedicated, described the sanctuary simply as "a two-story frame building," and the available pictorial evidence also suggests that the synagogue was modest in design and construction (see Figure 20). Nonetheless, the structure seems to have had a certain allure. Bern-

Figure 20. Bene Yeshurum, Chestnut Street, Paducah. This synagogue (indicated by the arrow) was built in 1871 and served until 1893. It is shown here on a section of H. Brosius's 1873 bird's-eye-view map of Paducah, in the Market House Museum, Paducah.

heim relates that it was seen as a "novelty" in Paducah and that the inauguration of the synagogue "attracted a large number of people who up to that time had never seen such a house of worship."[5] Both the austerity of the Bene Yeshurum synagogue and the interest it generated can be attributed largely to the fact that Paducah's Jewish community was quite new and very small when it built its first house of prayer. Only at the very end of the nineteenth century, when the community was better established and had begun to exhibit signs of growth, did it replace its original synagogue with a more substantial building.

The other synagogues erected in Kentucky during the latter decades of the nineteenth century were buildings with somewhat more character and greater longevity than Paducah's first meetinghouse. The Adath Israel synagogue of 1868, which replaced the structure that had burned in 1866, and the Brith Sholom synagogue of 1881, both in Louisville, were clearly influenced by the medieval revival styles that became firmly established in American ecclesiastical architecture in the period after the Civil War. Even the smaller Adas Israel synagogue in Henderson, dedicated in 1892, reveals the penchant of nineteenth-century architects and congregational building committees to adopt revival forms in the construction of their synagogues.

Figure 21. Adath Israel, Broadway and Sixth, Louisville. The grandest of Kentucky's nineteenth-century synagogues, this building served Adath Israel from 1868 until 1906 and was not torn down until 1942. From *History of Congregation Adath Israel, Louisville, Kentucky, and the Addresses Delivered at the Dedication of Its New Temple* (Louisville, 1906).

Adath Israel was an elaborate structure that mixed several styles. The central pointed arch and the finials at the top of the building were clearly Gothic in tone, while the rounded arches with hood moldings over the doorways and windows imparted an Italianate feeling (Figure 21). The Brith Sholom synagogue, like Adath Israel, was complex in design, and even more unusual in appearance. The primary influence on this building seems to have been Gothic; its dominant features were a large central pointed arch broken by two doorways and three lancet windows, and the three finials punctuating the upper reaches of its facade (Figure 22). The Adas Israel temple in Henderson is more unassuming than either of the two Louisville synagogues built in the second half of the nineteenth century (Henderson's Jewish community was even smaller than Paducah's), but Adas Israel too is somewhat complex

Figure 22. Brith Sholom, First Street, Louisville. This 1881 building, whose original facade is known today only from this poor-quality newsprint image, underwent substantial alterations after it passed to the Anshei Sfard congregation (see Figure 43). From *History of the Jews of Louisville, Ky.* (New Orleans, 1901).

in design. It features a simple Italianate tower at its corner, a series of pointed-arch Gothic windows along its sides, and a number of elements that seem to be derived from the Queen Anne style: a rounded exterior stairwell, molded brick above the doorway, a spindle ornament atop its tower (see Figure 23).

Figure 23. Adas Israel, Center Street, Henderson. Completed in 1892, this building incorporates design elements from several late nineteenth-century styles.

Surviving records from Kentucky's early Jewish congregations do not reveal much about the discussions that took place when they set about erecting their first synagogues, or about the kinds of design issues that must have arisen. This is unfortunate, since a synagogue community's decisions about how its building should look have such potential to reveal much about the congregation's collective self-image and internal dynamics. The few hints that do survive concerning debates over synagogue design are significant, however, for they often reveal intense disagreements within congregations, especially about the adoption of Reform practices. In 1849, for example, when the first Adath Israel building was consecrated in Louisville, "one of the members . . . threatened to burn down the Synagog if an organ were put in." And when Paducah's congregation inaugurated its first house of worship in 1871 "the question of family pews almost disrupted the little struggling organization."[6] Tantalizing revelations such as these make the paucity of information about the discussion of design issues even more frustrating.

There is also little information about the identity of the architects who designed Kentucky's early synagogues. This too is unfortunate, for whether members of a congregation were actively engaged in determining the design of their buildings or not, the architects with whom they chose to work must have had a great deal to do with the way these buildings looked in the end. Table 7, page 160, lists all the buildings constructed in Kentucky as synagogues over the years and, wherever possible, provides the names of the architects or architectural firms that designed them. For the first seven synagogues erected in the commonwealth, only one architect has been identified: H.P. Bradshaw, whose firm, known as Bradshaw and Brother, designed the 1868 Adath Israel building on Broadway in Louisville.

The architectural firm operated by H.P. Bradshaw and his brother Richard was perhaps the most important in Louisville in the third quarter of the nineteenth century. Several of Louisville's leading architects of the late nineteenth century passed through the Bradshaw office, and, in addition to Adath Israel, several important Gothic-style churches in Louisville have been attributed to the Bradshaw firm. These include St. John's Evangelical Church on East Market Street (1866), St. Louis Bertrand Roman Catholic Church on South Sixth Street (1871); and the First Unitarian Church on South Fourth Street (1872). The Bradshaws also built three schools for the city of Louisville. One of these, now called the Theodore Roosevelt School, is still standing on North Seventeenth Street.[7]

Whoever the designers of Kentucky's early synagogues were, it appears that they had some awareness of nineteenth-century trends in American synagogue design. Certainly the congregations that employed them must have given them some idea of their needs and must have made it clear that they considered the revival styles then being used in church and civic architecture appropriate for synagogue architecture as well.

One reason that styles frequently used in church design were so readily acceptable for American synagogues was that many American Jewish congregations in the late nineteenth and early twentieth centuries were making use of converted churches as their places of worship. In part, this occurred because many of America's congregations, often composed of immigrant families, could not afford new construction and it was also the case that changing residential patterns in late nineteenth- and early twentieth-century American cities created a ready supply of vacant church buildings. As the information in Table 5 indicates, the practice of using former church buildings as synagogues was rather widespread in Kentucky in the last years of the nineteenth century and the early years of the twentieth.

During the 1890s, former church buildings in Louisville were acquired by both the B'nai Jacob congregation and Adath Jeshurun (Figures 24 and 25). In 1903 the Brith Sholom congregation, having outgrown the synagogue it had built on Louisville's First Street, moved

Figure 24. B'nai Jacob, Jefferson Street, Louisville. This church (indicated by the arrow) was occupied by the B'nai Jacob congregation in the last decade of the nineteenth century and then replaced by a new building on the same site (see Figure 34). The church is shown here in J.T. Palmatary's 1855 bird's-eye-view map of Louisville. Photo by Tom Fougerousse.

into a building that was originally the College Street Presbyterian Church (Figure 26). In 1905 the United Hebrew Congregation in Newport moved into a former Christian church building (Figure 27), and that same year, by coincidence, two different Kentucky congregations acquired former German Lutheran churches to use as synagogues. These two congregations, whose acquisitions of buildings were discussed in Chapter 1, were the Orthodox Beth Hamedrash Hagodol in Louisville and the Reform Temple Adath Israel in Lexington (see Figures 6 and 8). In 1914, Lexington's Ohavay Zion moved into what had previously been a Presbyterian church, and in 1917 Louisville's Agudath Achim moved into a building that had been erected as St. John's Episcopal Church (see Figures 9 and 7).

A Jewish congregation that converted a church into its own place of worship generally did very little to alter the exterior other than to remove any explicitly Christian ornamentation and perhaps to add some indication of the building's new function. As Figure 26 reveals, Brith Sholom removed whatever Christian symbols may have adorned the archetypically Gothic revival structure it had bought and replaced

Figure 25. Adath Jeshurun, Chestnut Street, Louisville. Originally a Christian church, this building served as Adath Jeshurun's first home, from 1894 until 1919. It is pictured here as it appeared in 1921. From the University of Louisville Photographic Archives, Caufield and Shook Collection (neg. 40383).

them with a representation of the Ten Commandments over the door and a rather awkward looking Star of David at the peak of the roof. The first Adath Israel temple in Lexington apparently relied on nothing more than a wooden sign near its front door to indicate its identity as a Jewish place of worship (Figure 28); a metal plaque served a similar purpose at the first Ohavay Zion synagogue in the same city (Figure 29).

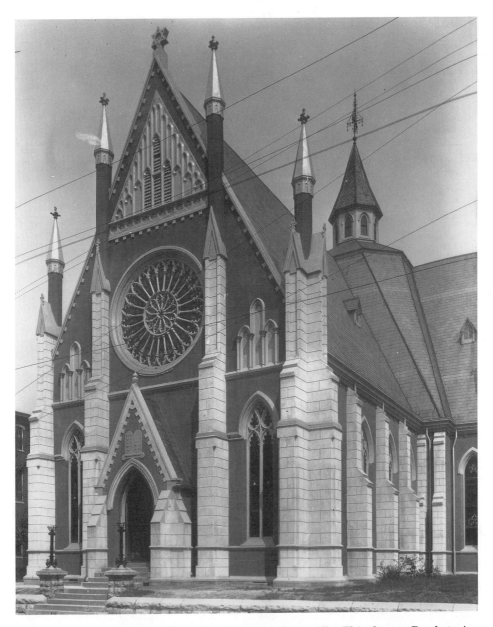

Figure 26. Brith Sholom, Second and College, Louisville. This former Presbyterian church served Brith Sholom from 1903 until 1950, when the congregation became the first to move from downtown to Louisville's Highlands neighborhood. From the University of Louisville Photographic Archives, Caufield and Shook Collection (neg. 28086).

Newport's United Hebrew Congregation placed a marker in the gable of its building bearing its name in both Hebrew and English.

Among the various historical styles adopted for newly constructed synagogues during the latter half of the nineteenth century, and still

Figure 27. United Hebrew Congregation, Fifth Street, Newport. Originally a church, this building served as an Orthodox synagogue for more than six decades and then became a church again. This picture was taken around 1940. Photograph by Myron Benson, courtesy of the Bureau of Jewish Education, Cincinnati, Ohio.

used occasionally in the twentieth, perhaps the most unusual was the so-called Moorish style with its bulbous domes, minarets, horseshoe arches, and extensive use of contrasting colors. Because it never became as popular for other buildings as it was for synagogues (most churches continued to be built in the Gothic or Romanesque modes), Moorish ecclesiastical architecture became increasingly associated with the Jewish faith. Although the Moorish style appealed to the romantic sentimentality of the later nineteenth century, like other medieval revival styles, it found special favor in the eyes of American Jewish congregations for other reasons as well.

Figure 28. The tablet that marked Adath Israel's Maryland Avenue sanctuary in Lexington. It is now on display at the congregation's Ashland Avenue temple. The letters K.K. before the name of the congregation stand for *kahal kadosh* meaning "holy assembly." Photograph courtesy of the Central Kentucky Jewish Federation, Lexington.

The popularity of Moorish architecture among Jewish congregations was certainly due in large part to the fact that it evoked certain memories of the Near Eastern origins of the Jewish faith. Moreover, it carried reminders of Judaism's Golden Age in Muslim Spain, when the country's Jewish minority was highly integrated into Spanish society and many individual Jews reached positions of great prominence. Its associations with a medieval Jewish community that blended well with

Figure 29. With an inscription reading "The first steps to happiness are the synagogue steps," this plaque marked Ohavay Zion's Maxwell Street synagogue in Lexington until 1986. It is now displayed at the congregation's Edgewater Court synagogue.

Figure 30. Adath Israel, Daviess Street, Owensboro. Constructed in 1877 and still serving as a Jewish house of worship, this small temple reflects the influence of Moorish design on American synagogues.

its surroundings made the Moorish style especially appealing to Reform congregations. To quote Michael Meyer, the foremost historian of Reform Judaism, the construction of Moorish synagogues seemed to be making a statement "that political and cultural integration did not require abdication of origins."[8]

Of course, the more Moorish architecture was embraced by prestigious Jewish congregations in the major cities of Europe and the United States, the more its adoption was encouraged in smaller communities. Its influence on synagogue design in Kentucky is best represented in the Adath Israel temple of Owensboro, constructed in 1877 and still standing as a National Historic Landmark (Figure 30), and in the Temple Israel building that was dedicated in Paducah in 1893 (Figure 31). The unique ornamentation atop the Owensboro temple and the

Figure 31. Temple Israel, Broadway and Seventh, Paducah. An imposing building constructed in 1893, this synagogue featured the Moorish domes that appeared on Jewish houses of worship in many parts of the United States in the late nineteenth century. Photo from a calendar for 1985-86, published by the Market House Museum, Paducah.

Figure 32. Paducah's Temple Israel after the Moorish domes were removed in the early 1930s. This is the way the building appeared until it was torn down in 1963. From Temple Israel confirmation booklet, *The Scroll* (Paducah, 1940).

marvelous onion domes of the Paducah structure mark these buildings unmistakably as houses of worship constructed during the heyday of Moorish synagogue design.

The architect of the Owensboro temple is not known, but the Paducah synagogue of 1893 was designed by Brinton B. Davis, a young architect who was then at the beginning of a productive career destined to last more than sixty years. Davis was born in Natchez, Mississippi, and, after serving an apprenticeship in New York he came to Kentucky in 1890 to work on a model industrial town at Grand Rivers. When his work on that project was completed, he settled in Paducah and remained there for about ten years. In 1902, with his reputation well established, he moved to Louisville; one of the many commissions he received in the city was the design of the Bowling Green campus of Western Kentucky University, a project on which he worked throughout the years from 1909 to 1939. Davis cited the Paducah temple as one of his major accomplishments when he applied for fellowship in the American Institute of Architects in 1897, but since no detailed records of this project have survived, we cannot be certain why he chose to build it in the Moorish style. A notice published in Paducah in 1894, however, observes that "to Rev. Morris Ungerleider, the present rabbi, is due the credit of inspiring his people to build this temple," and it is certainly likely that it was Rabbi Ungerleider who suggested a Moorish motif to Davis.[9]

Neither the Paducah temple nor its smaller counterpart in Owensboro were of purely Moorish design, of course. Even a glance at the Owensboro building reveals that its doorway and windows are Gothic in character, and the central window and front archways of the Paducah synagogue have a Romanesque feel. Indeed, when the three main domes of the Paducah temple were removed in the mid-1930s (one long-time resident of the city reports that this was done because of problems with roosting pigeons), the building lost much of its Moorish appearance. Still, the horseshoe arches at the upper reaches of the temple and the miniature onion domes flanking the central window remained as reminders of the Moorish theme that had inspired much of the building's original design (see Figure 32).

Although the Owensboro and Paducah temples were the Kentucky synagogues that most clearly reflected Moorish influence, something of this Mediterranean style had also been introduced into the multifaceted 1868 Adath Israel building in Louisville. Of special interest in this regard are the elongated domes atop the twin towers of the Louisville temple, domes whose design was mimicked atop the ark that dominated the Adath Israel interior (see Figure 33). It may be significant that late in 1866, at the same time that the members of Adath Israel's Building and Finance Committee were negotiating with H.P. Bradshaw about a design for their new temple, the board dispatched several individuals to

Figure 33. Interior of the Adath Israel temple at Broadway and Sixth, Louisville, as it appeared around 1905. Judging from the decoration of the sanctuary with greenery, this photograph was taken during the festival of Shavuot. From *History of Congregation Adath Israel, Louisville, Kentucky, and the Addresses Delivered at the Dedication of its New Temple* (Louisville, 1906).

Cincinnati to "get plans from the Temples erected there."[10] During their visit to Cincinnati these gentlemen must have inspected the newly constructed Plum Street temple designed by the local architect James K. Wilson. The Plum Street temple, still standing, was one of the earliest American synagogues to utilize Islamic motifs and is considered a classic example of the Moorish genre. It is not unlikely that Adath Israel's building committee discussed this innovative Cincinnati synagogue with Bradshaw.

Also bearing a hint of the Moorish influence was the synagogue dedicated by B'nai Jacob in 1901. The Moorish flavor of this structure, constructed on the Jefferson Street site of the former church that B'nai Jacob had occupied during the previous decade, was imparted by the use of alternating courses of light and dark brick in the towers of an otherwise essentially Romanesque structure (see Figure 34).

Ultimately, of course, neither Italianate nor Romanesque nor even Moorish synagogues could be perceived as buildings of inherently Jew-

Figure 34. B'nai Jacob, Jefferson Street, Louisville. This building was dedicated in 1901 on the site of a former church that had served as B'nai Jacob's synagogue from 1891 (see Figure 24). Photo courtesy of Keneseth Israel Congregation.

Figure 35. Adath Israel, Third Street, Louisville. This neoclassical building, dedicated in 1906, served Adath Israel until 1977. Photo from the University of Louisville Photographic Archives, Caufield and Shook Collection (neg. 44072).

ish design, and Gothic motifs came to be seen as particularly inappropriate for synagogues, given their close association with medieval Christianity. Moreover, many of the synagogue buildings of the nineteenth century could be criticized for making indiscriminate use of several styles at once. As the British architect and author Edward Jamilly has observed in reference to both Europe and America, "It was by no means unusual to find, in the same synagogue building, forms and details drawn from half a dozen historical styles of architecture and mixed together with remarkable lack of taste and consistency."[11] Thus American synagogue architecture (like church architecture) continued to evolve in the twentieth century. For one thing, there was something of a revival of neoclassical design in American synagogue architecture, stimulated in part by a similar neoclassical interest on the part of church architects and in part by recent archaeological discoveries of Greco-Roman synagogue remains in Palestine.

In Louisville, the renewed interest in neoclassicism was best represented in the new temple that Adath Israel dedicated in 1906 (Figure 35). There had been talk of building a new temple for the congregation in the very first years of the twentieth century, but a decision to do so was not taken until some of the stucco work at Adath Israel's Broadway temple collapsed in February of 1904. The congregation held its services in Brith Sholom's temple for a while, and at the same time it searched for a new building site and launched an elaborate competition to select a design for a new synagogue. Entries were submitted by at least five architects, including Brinton Davis, who had designed Paducah's 1893 Temple Israel, and William G. Tachau of the New York firm of Pilcher and Tachau, who would later publish an important essay on the history and theory of American synagogue architecture.[12] The winning submission, however, was that of McDonald and Sheblessy, a partnership of two of Louisville's most accomplished turn-of-the-century architects.

Kenneth McDonald was one of several brothers who had migrated to Kentucky from Virginia just after the Civil War to establish what soon became one of nineteenth-century Louisville's premier architectural firms. McDonald Brothers stayed in operation until 1895, and after it dissolved, Kenneth worked in design and construction on his own for a few years. Then, in 1901, he joined forces with John Francis Sheblessy, who had recently come to Louisville from Chicago. Among McDonald and Sheblessy's early projects were the Second English Lutheran Church on West Jefferson Street in Louisville, and the Kentucky Building at the 1904 World's Fair in St. Louis.

Adath Israel was probably McDonald and Sheblessy's last commission, for the short-lived partnership was dissolved around 1905. John Sheblessy was to leave Louisville in 1907 for Cincinnati, where he would undertake several architectural projects for the Catholic Church. Kenneth McDonald stayed in Louisville, however, and formed a new partnership with William J. Dodd, who was, like Sheblessy, a Chicago-trained architect. Dodd, whose own plan for Adath Israel had been rejected in the temple's 1904 competition, had previously been in a partnership with Arthur Cobb. It was the firm of Dodd and Cobb that had designed the 1898 addition to the old Adath Israel building at Sixth and Broadway and other important projects in Louisville as well, including the Presbyterian Theological Seminary on Broadway (now Jefferson Community College) and the renowned Seelbach Hotel.[13]

The extent to which McDonald and Sheblessy had specifically Jewish considerations in mind when they designed Adath Israel is unknown. There is no way of determining whether they were aware of recent Greco-Roman synagogue discoveries in Palestine, for example, or how important it was that a member of the congregation, Alfred Joseph, served as senior draftsman on the project. What is clear, however, is that in adopting McDonald and Sheblessy's striking neoclassical design, Adath Israel was attempting to associate itself with the most sophisticated artistic sentiment of the time and the latest developments in American culture. In doing so, the commonwealth's oldest congregation

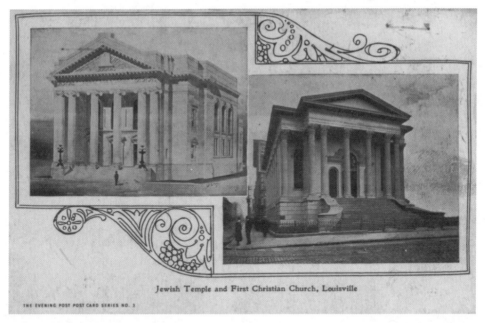

Jewish Temple and First Christian Church, Louisville

THE EVENING POST POST CARD SERIES NO. 3

Figure 36. Temple Adath Israel and the First Christian Church in Louisville, shown on a turn-of-the-century postcard. The pairing of these two buildings reveals the frequent architectural similarity between American synagogues and churches. The drawing of Adath Israel shows tablets of the Ten Commandments that did not appear in the pediment of the actual building. Courtesy of Wade Hall.

was declaring its strong sense of self-confidence and its feeling of security as a part of Kentucky society. The resemblance of Adath Israel's new building to other important structures in Louisville's architectural environment was no doubt intended, and it was not lost on local observers (see Figure 36). Moreover, in choosing the design of its new temple, Adath Israel was proclaiming the substantial material success of its members; when he symbolically handed the key of the new temple over to the congregation's president, the chairman of Adath Israel's building committee urged his fellow congregants to "come forward with a prayer of thanksgiving to the kind Providence who has blessed us with the freedom of this country, and a goodly portion of this world's goods."[14]

Besides a revived interest in neoclassicism, another important development that can be observed in early twentieth-century synagogue architecture is the appearance of large-domed, centrally focused sanctuaries based on Byzantine designs. Like nineteenth-century Moorish synagogues, Byzantine synagogues evoked certain Mediterranean associations, and like the revival of neoclassicism, the use of Byzantine forms may have been linked to early twentieth-century archaeological discoveries in Palestine. Moreover, the use of a domed central plan, rather than an axial plan, was well suited to synagogues that were

Figure 37. Adath Jeshurun, Brook Street, Louisville. This Byzantine style structure was erected in 1919 and served Adath Jeshurun until 1957. From the University of Louisville Photographic Archives, Caufield and Shook Collection (neg. 37570).

trying to maintain something of the sense of congregational cohesion that had characterized the traditional arrangement of synagogue interiors. The social critic Lewis Mumford went so far as to recommend that Jewish congregations adopt the domed Byzantine style as the standard form for their synagogues, arguing that "if it were possible for the dome to be used consistently in synagog architecture in America, a very definite step would be taken towards a coherent architectural style, which would give the stamp of Judaism to a synagog, as plainly as the baroque gives the stamp of the Jesuit order to a church."[15]

Only a single synagogue in Kentucky was built in the Byzantine style, but it is a striking example of the genre, and its existence serves as a nice reminder that even among the limited number of Jewish houses of worship constructed in the Bluegrass State, there is at least one representative of every major architectural style that has influenced American synagogue design in the last century and a half. Kentucky's single example of a domed synagogue in the Byzantine mode is the 1919 Adath Jeshurun building on Brook Street in Louisville (Figure 37), designed by James J. Gaffney. Although Gaffney himself was a devoted Catholic (when he died without heirs in 1946, he left substantial bequests to several Catholic institutions), his selection as the architect for Adath Jeshurun was a brilliant choice.

Gaffney had already made a name for himself as a first-rate designer even before World War I, and among his most impressive buildings were two notable Roman Catholic churches still standing in Louisville: the Holy Name Church on Third Street, and the St. James Church on Bardstown Road, both completed around 1913. In constructing these sanctuaries, Gaffney demonstrated his skill with the kinds of features he would later integrate into Adath Jeshurun's synagogue: the incorporation of mosaic work, the use of light-colored brick, the focus on a dome. Perhaps it was the Adath Jeshurun building committee's familiarity with Gaffney's work in the Byzantine style that attracted its members to him. Unfortunately, the only record of the congregation's selection process is a brief note recorded in the minutes of the board of directors: "Bldg Com made a report that Mr. Gafney drawing was presented and his proposition was acceptable."[16]

Although the popularity of certain synagogue styles waxed and waned over the years, it should be stressed that throughout the decades before World War II, synagogues all over the United States continued to be built in a wide variety of forms. Indeed, twentieth-century architects, like their nineteenth-century predecessors, often drew upon several traditions in the same building, again with varying degrees of success. The synagogues built in several smaller Kentucky cities between the beginning of World War I and the outbreak of World War II attest to the multiplicity of styles employed in American synagogue construction.

The first Jewish house of worship in Covington, for example, was designed as an uncomplicated neoclassical structure centered on a pair of Tuscan columns (see Figure 38). This building, erected in 1915 for the Temple of Israel congregation, was the work of George W. Schofield, a forty-two-year-old architect who had been practicing locally since 1898. Hopkinsville's modest Adath Israel synagogue of 1925 was also neoclassical in tone, with simple columns and a triangular pediment (see Figure 39). The Hopkinsville building was apparently the work of an amateur designer rather than a trained architect; it seems to have been planned by Wolf Geller, a merchant who had come to Hopkinsville from Evansville, Indiana, around 1912. According to Geller's daughter, he patterned the Hopkinsville synagogue after the one in which he had worshiped in Evansville, and he spent more than a year supervising the construction himself.

In contrast to the small neoclassical synagogues in Covington and Hopkinsville, the 1926 Adath Israel temple in Lexington was built in an essentially Romanesque style, even though the columns that flank its entry are topped by Corinthian capitals (Figure 40). The architect was Leon K. Frankel, a Louisville native who had studied at the University

Figure 38. Temple of Israel, Seventh Street, Covington. This drawing of Covington's first synagogue, in the collection of the American Jewish Archives, Cincinnati, was prepared in 1915 by the building's architect, George W. Schofield.

Figure 39. Adath Israel, Sixth Street, Hopkinsville. This building, constructed in 1925, was demolished in 1977 after its roof collapsed under a heavy snow. From William T. Turner, comp., *A Pictorial History of Hopkinsville and Christian County since 1865*, vol. 2 of *Gate Way from the Past* (Hopkinsville, Ky., 1974).

Figure 40. Adath Israel, Ashland Avenue, Lexington. This 1926 temple built in a predominantly Romanesque style was designed by Lexington architect L.K. Frankel, a member of the congregation.

of Kentucky and had returned there to teach. Frankel served as professor of design at the university until 1919 and then founded the firm of Frankel and Curtis with his U.K. colleague, John J. Curtis, a professor of engineering. Frankel became a member of the prestigious American Institute of Architects in the same year his Adath Israel project was completed, and he was considered one of Lexington's leading architects in the interwar period. Only a few years after Kentucky passed a law regulating the profession of architecture, for example, Frankel was appointed to the State Board of Examiners and Registration of Architects; he served from 1935 to 1947.[17]

George Schofield's Temple of Israel building in Covington was replaced by a new synagogue just before World War II. The new sanctuary, designed by Leslie Moss and dedicated in 1939, can best be described as a functional building with little personality (Figure 41). Moss, a native of Liverpool, England, had come to the United States at the age of six and in 1932 had established an architectural firm with his brother in Cincinnati. In his design for the Covington synagogue, Moss was very likely constrained by the fact that the building was commissioned in the midst of the Great Depression. Indeed, the Temple of Israel congregation probably would not have been able to build a new sanctuary at all had not the federal government bought its old synagogue property in

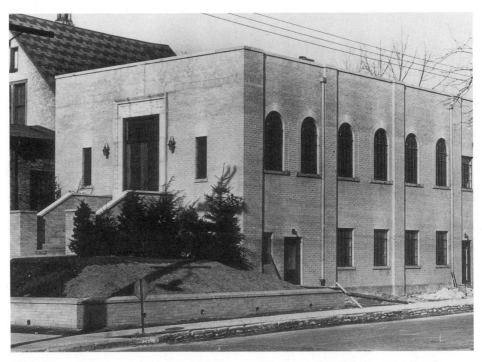

Figure 41. Temple of Israel, Scott Street, Covington. This functional building was dedicated by the congregation in 1939 after its first sanctuary was torn down to make way for Covington's post office. Photograph courtesy of the Bureau of Jewish Education, Cincinnati, Ohio.

Figure 42. Agudath Achim, Montgomery Avenue, Ashland. This Reform temple, built in 1938, became a church when organized Jewish life ceased in Ashland around 1986.

Figure 43. Anshei Sfard, First Street, Louisville. Anshei Sfard acquired the former Brith Sholom building in 1903 and in 1928 added a new wing to the structure, tying its old and new elements together with the dramatic facade shown here. From the University of Louisville Photographic Archives, R.G. Potter Collection (neg. 4092).

order to make way for a new post office. The other Jewish house of worship erected in Kentucky during the Great Depression is the nondescript Agudath Achim building in Ashland, perhaps the least handsome of all the commonwealth's pre–World War II synagogues (Figure 42).

The synagogues of Louisville, like those of Kentucky's smaller Jewish communities, also reflect the variety of architectural influences at work in the interwar period. The new facade added to Anshei Sfard's First Street building in 1928 made use of arabesque patterns that imparted an exotic, perhaps Moorish, feeling to the structure (Figure 43), whereas Keneseth Israel's 1929 building is fundamentally neoclassical in style, dominated as it is by two-story Corinthian columns (Fig-

Figure 44. The Keneseth Israel building, Jacob Street, Louisville, as it appeared in the early 1990s. Like the other two synagogue buildings still standing in downtown Louisville, it is on the National Register of Historic Places and now serves as a church.

ure 44). The designer of the Anshei Sfard facade is unknown, but the Keneseth Israel building was the work of Joseph and Joseph, an architectural firm established by Alfred Joseph and his brother Oscar in 1908, soon after Alfred had finished working as senior draftsman on Adath Israel's Third Street building. Joseph and Joseph's Keneseth Israel is now listed on the National Register of Historic Places, as are the other two synagogue buildings still standing in downtown Louisville, McDonald and Sheblessy's Adath Israel and James J. Gaffney's Adath Jeshurun.

Despite the variety of architectural styles apparent in Kentucky's nineteenth- and early twentieth-century synagogues, many of them share a number of exterior design elements. It was not uncommon, for example, for Kentucky's pre–World War II synagogues to bear prominent inscriptions on their facades. Photographs from the half-century before World War II reveal that early synagogues marked with the names of their congregations could be found in Louisville, Newport,

Hopkinsville, Lexington, Ashland, and Covington. Others had facades emblazoned not with a name, but with some other appropriate inscription. On Owensboro's Adath Israel is etched the quotation "This is the gateway to the Lord, they shall enter through it." This text is obviously based on Psalms 118:20, which reads "This is the gateway to the Lord, the righteous shall enter through it." Why the word "righteous" was omitted from the inscription is a mystery; perhaps it was done in the name of inclusiveness. Louisville's Adath Israel temple on Third Street also bears a biblical inscription, this one taken from Isaiah 56:7 and rendered in a rather florid translation: "Mine house shall be an house of prayer for all people."

Although the evidence available is very limited, Hebrew seems to have been the language of choice for nineteenth-century synagogue inscriptions in Kentucky, perhaps because early Jewish immigrants to America were still likely to be proficient readers of Hebrew texts. The inscription on Louisville's 1857 Beth Israel and the quotation on Owensboro's 1877 Adath Israel are both in Hebrew, for example. By the early twentieth century, however, English had made its appearance alongside Hebrew in synagogue inscriptions and in some cases supplanted it entirely, especially on the buildings of Reform congregations that were making a conscious effort to blend into their surroundings. The ecumenical quotation from Isaiah on the 1906 Adath Israel building appears only in English, for instance, and over the doorways of the Reform temples in Lexington and in Ashland are etched only the English legends "Adath Israel Temple" and "Agudath Achim Temple."

Besides the use of prominent inscriptions, another practice common in many of Kentucky's early synagogues and temples was the installation of stained glass windows. These often incorporated Jewish symbols such as the Star of David, the menorah, and the tablets of the Ten Commandments, or designs related to various biblical or holiday themes. Sometimes synagogue windows carried the names of individuals to whom they were dedicated or of individuals or families who contributed money to have them installed, either at the time the synagogue was built or in later years. A text from one window in the Owensboro temple is representative: "In Memory of Rabbi David Feuerlicht—Born May 25, 1850, Died August 3, 1896."

Notably rare in Kentucky synagogue windows (and in synagogue art more generally) is any depiction of the human form. The general absence of representational art in the synagogue is a consequence of the biblical prohibition against making any image or likeness of a human being or an animal, expressed most clearly in Exodus 20:4 and in Deuteronomy 4:16–18 and 5:8. The prohibition is quite forcefully stated in these passages, and over the centuries it was reinforced in some communities by a concern that representational art in the synagogue might be a distraction to worshipers. Nonetheless, the context in which

Figure 45. A stained glass window featuring a menorah, from Owensboro's Adath Israel temple.

Figure 46. A series of stained glass windows featuring Stars of David and tablets of the Ten Commandments, from Adath Jeshurun's 1919 building in Louisville.

the biblical injunctions concerning "graven images" is uttered suggests that the ban was intended to apply specifically to the making of images for worship, and so rabbinic attitudes toward figurative art have always been somewhat ambivalent. Often the prohibition has been significantly relaxed, even where the plastic arts are concerned, and depictions of animals (especially lions) have come to be widely accepted as decorative elements in ritual settings. Still, traditional Jews have retained a certain reluctance to represent the human form, and so the likelihood of finding decoration or ornamentation incorporating human figures is much greater in Reform temples than in other synagogues.

Among the pre–World War II Kentucky synagogues that were adorned with windows using Judaic motifs were the Adath Israel temple in Owensboro (see Figure 45), the 1919 Adath Jeshurun building in Louisville (see Figure 46), and the 1929 Keneseth Israel building, also in Louisville (the Judaic emblems were removed from the Keneseth Israel windows when the building was sold in 1964, but they have apparently been lost). The Agudath Achim temple in Ashland also features some rather pleasing stained glass. But certainly the most spectacular examples of stained glass windows surviving in a pre–World War II Kentucky synagogue are the three in Louisville's 1906 Adath Israel temple, now the Greater Bethel Apostolic Church. These windows are striking not only because of their fine craftsmanship but also because of their dramatic departure from the long-standing aversion to the depiction of individual personalities in synagogue art (see Figure 47).

Figure 47. A stained glass window from Adath Israel's Third Street Temple in Louisville. The figure depicted is Abraham.

Figure 48. The distinctive facade of the old Ohavay Zion synagogue on Maxwell Street in Lexington, shown on a T-shirt worn by the author's son. The stained glass window once associated with Ohavay Zion has become the logo of the Italian restaurant now housed in the building.

Figure 49. Interior of Adath Israel on Third Street in Louisville as it appeared in the early 1990s. The organ dominating the front of the hall clearly indicates this synagogue was built for a Reform congregation.

Of course, stained glass also featured prominently in synagogues that had formerly been churches. There are no known cases of a Kentucky Jewish congregation removing the stained glass windows from a church that it had acquired (though it would have done so if the windows had contained designs inappropriate for a synagogue), and several churches-turned-synagogues in Kentucky retained notable examples of stained glass artistry—for example, the first buildings of both Adath Israel and Ohavay Zion in Lexington (see Figures 8 and 9). Indeed, the prominent stained glass window of the Ohavay Zion facade became something of a symbol of the building, and that symbol has been given new life recently as the logo of the Italian restaurant that now occupies the former sanctuary (see Figure 48).

Unfortunately, there is even less visual evidence of the interiors of Kentucky's earliest synagogues than of their outward appearance. The paucity of information about Kentucky's two pre–Civil War synagogues has already been mentioned, and there is just as little about some of the other buildings that served Kentucky Jewry in the late nineteenth and early twentieth centuries. Of the twenty-six buildings that served as synagogues at one time or another before World War II, only eleven are still standing, and only two of these are still functioning as Jewish houses of worship: the Adath Israel temples in Owensboro and in Lexington.

Of course, the present interior of a former synagogue can provide some idea of how it looked in the past. Most of the surviving buildings that served as synagogues in the prewar era have not undergone any major interior reconstruction. Turn-of-the-century pipe organs are still in place in the former Adas Israel temple in Henderson, for example, and also in the former Adath Israel sanctuary on Third Street in Louisville (see Figure 49), although neither of these instruments is in working order. Some Kentucky churches that were once synagogues have even retained the Judaic symbols and the Hebrew inscriptions that they inherited. At the Greater Bethel Apostolic Church, the Ten Commandments still appear in both English and Hebrew on the front wall of the sanctuary, and the verses "Hear O Israel the Lord our God the Lord is One" in English and "The Lord is God" in Hebrew still appear in gold lettering over the ark where Torah scrolls were once arrayed. At Louisville's Unity Temple, formerly the home of congregation Adath Jeshurun, the dome is still adorned with a giant Star of David, and the same symbol is integrated into the capitals of all the interior pillars (see Figure 50).

Even when changes have been made by a synagogue's new owners, it is often possible to see beyond these alterations and to learn something about the earlier appearance of the building. At the former Agudath Achim temple in Ashland, for instance, the twelve lights around the ark niche, originally representing the twelve tribes of Israel,

Figure 50. The capital of a column decorated with a Star of David from the interior of the Adath Jeshurun synagogue on Brook Street in Louisville.

are still present, though the alcove itself now contains a depiction of Jesus and the lights are said to represent the twelve apostles. At the old Keneseth Israel building in Louisville, now the Calvary Cathedral, the ark that once held Torah scrolls is still in place, though the images of two doves are now suspended by wires within it and the inscription "Jesus is Here" appears above it.

Still, the present layouts of former synagogues can hardly be completely reliable guides to what their interiors were like in the past.

Figure 51. The Ten Commandments in the form of a book, perhaps the only tangible artifact remaining from the Agudath Achim synagogue in Louisville. It is now on display at the Hillel Jewish Student Center at the University of Cincinnati.

Perhaps most significantly, the *bimah* areas in several former synagogues have been completely redesigned and rebuilt by the Christian congregations that took them over, often to accommodate choirs and instrumental groups at the front of the hall. Among the former synagogues whose pulpit areas have been radically transformed are the 1892 Adas Israel building in Henderson, the 1906 Adath Israel building in Louisville, and the original Keneseth Israel building, also in Louisville. The interior of the former Ohavay Zion synagogue in Lexington was completely remodeled when it became a restaurant, and what was once the *bimah* in the sanctuary is today the eatery's bar area!

Attempts to become acquainted with the appearance of Kentucky's early synagogues are also hindered by the scarcity of pictures portraying the original interior designs of these buildings. In the case of pre–World War II synagogues that have already disappeared or have undergone significant renovation, sometimes the only physical reminders of the way their interiors looked are a few remnants that have been salvaged and preserved (see, for example, Figure 51). Nonetheless, on the basis of whatever physical evidence has survived, the recollections of elders in the community, and certain reasonable assumptions, it is possible to make some observations about the interiors of Kentucky's late nineteenth- and early twentieth-century synagogues.

We can assume, for instance, that the commonwealth's Orthodox congregations in the nineteenth century and in the first half of the twentieth century retained separate seating arrangements for men and women, and that they organized the worship space around or behind a *bimah* on which the main reader's table faced forward, toward the ark. If any of Kentucky's early traditional synagogues had lecterns facing the congregation, these were of secondary importance and were not the focus of attention during most of the synagogue service. Oral testimony suggests that at least one Louisville synagogue, Beth Hamedrash Hagodol, had a *bimah* in the center of the sanctuary, completely surrounded by seating, and that in Hopkinsville there was a dispute over the placement of the *bimah* at the time the Adath Israel synagogue was being erected. It seems that some of the town's more traditional families wanted the *bimah* to stand in the center of the sanctuary, but Wolf Geller, who supervised the construction of the building, insisted that it be positioned at the front of the hall.

Certain assumptions can likewise be made about the commonwealth's Reform temples. One can speculate, for example, that very early in their existence, Reform congregations adopted mixed seating and arranged their pulpits so that lecterns were oriented toward the congregation, rather than toward the ark of the Torah. The nineteenth-century temple buildings in Owensboro and Henderson, both of which still have their original pulpit furnishings, bear witness to the early adoption in Reform temples of interiors similar to those of churches (see

Figure 52. The interior of Owensboro's Adath Israel temple as it appeared in the early 1990s.

Figure 52). The arrangement of Lexington's Adath Israel temple is also based upon the placement of the lectern facing the congregation and the use of family pews (see Figure 53).

Figure 53. The interior of Lexington's Adath Israel as it appeared in the early 1990s.

Figure 54. The interior of the Keneseth Israel synagogue around 1960, showing the free-standing *bimah*. Photo courtesy of Keneseth Israel Congregation.

The few extant photographs showing the interiors of Kentucky's pre–World War II synagogues tend to confirm the foregoing conjectures. For example, a particularly valuable photo of the 1929 Keneseth Israel sanctuary, taken from what was originally the women's gallery, clearly shows a synagogue interior designed with Orthodox practice in mind (see Figure 54). The *bimah* is a freestanding element with a reader's table facing in the same direction as the seats; at the front of the hall before the ark is a separate raised rostrum on which various dignitaries could be seated. A photograph of the modest Temple of Israel synagogue in Covington, though too poor in quality to reproduce, shows a common variant on the traditional interior arrangement. The *bimah* of this Orthodox *shul* serves both as the officiant's platform and as the rostrum before the ark, but the reader's table faces toward the ark rather than the congregation. The photograph also shows the synagogue's *mechitza*, a low curtain dividing the men's and women's seating areas.

The interior of Louisville's First Street synagogue, erected by Brith Sholom and used later by Anshei Sfard, deserves special mention. In its original design, Brith Sholom apparently chose an arrangement of *bimah* and seats designed for a service in which the officiant faced the congregation. The Orthodox Anshei Sfard congregation that acquired this building at the beginning of the twentieth century, however, adapted it to a more traditional arrangement of the worship space. The

Figure 55. The *bimah* of the First Street *shul* in Louisville as it appeared around 1955. Photograph by Gus Frank on deposit at Congregation Anshei Sfard.

congregation's compromise was to leave in place the existing lectern at the front of the *bimah*, facing the congregation, but to add at the center of the *bimah* a second reader's table facing the ark (the table is not shown in Figure 55). It was from the table facing the ark that the Torah was read and the service conducted.

The history of Louisville's First Street synagogue provides a powerful reminder of how revealing the physical appearance of a congregation's house of worship can be. In the year that the United States entered World War II, the First Street synagogue was exactly sixty years old, and during the six decades of its existence the look of its exterior and the organization of its interior had been crucial matters about which two different congregations had made decisions. In opting for an essentially Gothic design and a churchlike interior when it commissioned the building, Brith Sholom had revealed a lot about its evolving identity. In the same way, Anshei Sfard had said a great deal about its character when it altered the structure of the First Street synagogue by adding a second reader's table on the *bimah*, constructing a women's section for the sanctuary, and erecting a rather exotic external facade. In Kentucky synagogues of the period since World War II, issues of design and appearance remained extremely significant.

Chapter 4

Synagogue Design since World War II

THE YEARS IMMEDIATELY AFTER World War II marked a major watershed in American synagogue construction, for as Jews all over America migrated from the central city and out to the suburbs, it only made sense for their congregations to follow them and for new synagogues to be built in those neighborhoods that were attracting large numbers of Jewish families. The migration of Jews from downtown Louisville to the Highlands was reflected in the relocation of that city's congregations at midcentury. At the same time, moreover, membership rolls were growing, and this too served as a stimulus for synagogue construction. Congregational membership grew in the postwar era because synagogues, like churches, were increasingly seen as centers of social interaction that could provide a sense of community in the developing suburban milieu. Indeed, church or synagogue membership became almost a requirement for social respectability among the new middle-class suburbanites of the 1950s and 1960s. The twin factors of congregational relocation and increased religious affiliation combined to prompt the construction of more than 500 new synagogue buildings in the United States between the years 1945 and 1965.[1]

The architects who designed the new suburban synagogues and temples that went up all over the country after World War II abandoned almost completely the historical styles that had dominated American synagogue design for so many decades. Instead, architects working for Jewish congregations, like many working for Christian assemblies, began to adapt for ecclesiastical use a contemporary building style that had no inherent religious associations. The best known and most admired synagogue buildings of the immediate postwar era were those that took advantage of parklike settings and employed the most innovative design ideas and structural techniques of the period. Borrowing from the functionalism that had emerged in the interwar era (and whose influence could be seen even in a few synagogues of the 1930s), the designers of postwar American synagogues created buildings whose exteriors were generally clean, even austere, and whose surfaces were largely devoid of ornamentation. Writing in 1966, the American commentator on synagogue art Avram Kampf observed that "modern architecture was adopted because it admirably suited the needs of the community. It held the promise of efficiency, rationality, economy, order and a fresh start."[2]

Although not all postwar synagogues were equally successful as creative endeavors, the imaginative designs of well-known architects such as Eric Mendelsohn, Percival Goodman, and Frank Lloyd Wright helped to establish the dominance of a contemporary style in the years just after World War II, and the new approach represented by these masters has been widely accepted as the basis for synagogue architecture throughout the second half of the twentieth century. As early as 1954 the Union of American Hebrew Congregations (UAHC), the umbrella organization of Reform Judaism, published a book promoting the new postwar approach.

Titled *An American Synagogue for Today and Tomorrow,* the volume contained articles by more than three dozen contributors, including several world-class architects and a number of leading rabbis. In the introduction, Rabbi Maurice N. Eisendrath, then president of the UAHC, bemoaned the fact that "frequently we cannot be sure as we pass a synagogue whether it is a mosque, a Greek or Roman temple, or even a Gothic shrine of Christendom, to say nothing of a high school or a theater." Like others before him, he protested that "mere mimicry of the architectural forms developed by the faiths of others" would not do in synagogue design, and he proclaimed *An American Synagogue for Today and Tomorrow* "the first definitive volume on contemporary synagogue architecture."

Included in the UAHC volume were articles on the history of the synagogue since biblical times, on practical matters such as site selection and choosing an architect, on the planning of various parts of the building, and on the incorporation of art and music. The book also had sections describing several American synagogues built in the years immediately after World War II, and it dealt with such mundane matters as lighting, heating, ventilation, and legal protection. The overall purpose of the volume, its editor declared, was "nothing less than to lay the foundation for a great renaissance in the architecture of the synagogue."[3]

Given what was happening to synagogue design on a national level in the decades immediately after the Second World War, it is not surprising that all the synagogues built in Kentucky in the second half of the twentieth century, with the exception of the Georgian-style Brith Sholom building of the early 1950s (Figure 56), exhibit a decidedly

Figure 56. Brith Sholom, Cowling Avenue, Louisville. Brith Sholom erected its social hall and then its sanctuary in the early 1950s on the grounds of a nineteenth-century mansion (see Figure 15). This building is the only Kentucky synagogue of the second half of the twentieth century not designed in a modern architectural style. Rendering on the cover of *Dedication Service: Congregation B'rith Sholom* (Louisville, 1956).

modern style. Modern architects have often thought of their buildings as complete works of art in themselves, creations that needed little or no additional embellishment, and so late twentieth-century synagogues have often been designed with little or no external ornamentation. The kinds of inscriptions that were once common on synagogue exteriors have largely disappeared. Keneseth Israel and The Temple are notable for the attractively landscaped markers on their front lawns (see Figure 57), but of the seven synagogues built in Kentucky since 1950, only Louisville's Anshei Sfard has its name emblazoned on its facade (though Lexington's Ohavay Zion does have its name over its lobby entrance),

Figure 57. Landscaped marker on the lawn of Keneseth Israel in Louisville. Several post–World War II Kentucky synagogues are identified by such markers.

Figure 58. Temple Israel, Joe Clifton Drive, Paducah. The third synagogue building of the local Jewish congregation, this structure, like several others in Kentucky, is identified as a Jewish house of worship by the menorah on its facade.

and only Adath Jeshurun has a biblical quotation on its exterior, a rather inconspicuously carved selection from Psalms 119:105, in both Hebrew and English: "Thy word is a lamp unto my feet."

Still, the ongoing search for a way to stamp a synagogue as a distinctively Jewish building could not be abandoned in the postwar era, and since the middle of the century there has been a tendency to identify America's new suburban synagogues by marking their fronts with some sort of prominent symbol of Judaism, a symbol consciously integrated into its architectural surroundings and often a substantial work of art in itself. The symbol is sometimes representational, sometimes abstract; sometimes based on an individual artist's conception of a theme from the Jewish tradition, sometimes a version of a standard Jewish emblem such as the Star of David or the tablets of the Ten Commandments. In Kentucky, the Jewish symbol most commonly employed has been the seven-branched menorah: it appears in colored glass at Anshei Sfard, in metal piping at Temple Israel in Paducah (Figure 58), in poured concrete at The Temple, and as a transom design crafted by a congregant at Temple Shalom (Figure 59). Some of these compositions are worthy of notice as works of art in their own right, but the appearance of the menorah on so many Kentucky synagogue facades suggests that congregations of every sort were following the same basic formula in identifying their buildings as Jewish houses of worship.

Figure 59. Temple Shalom, Lowe Road, Louisville. This synagogue, designed by Louisville architect Gerald Baron, was dedicated in 1989. Both a menorah and a Star of David are featured prominently in its design.

Of course, not only aesthetic considerations but more mundane practical concerns as well have helped determine how postwar synagogues would look. Avram Kampf, reviewing twenty years of postwar synagogue design, was even moved to lament that "architects have frequently sacrificed expression to function" and to complain that many of their buildings did not convey "any sense of the cultural and religious meaning of Judaism."[4] Among the basic factors that have influenced synagogue design since the late 1940s, in Kentucky as elsewhere, one of the most important has been the changing pattern of synagogue attendance.

Within the immigrant generation that dominated American Jewish religious life until the interwar period, there was a significant proportion of religiously knowledgeable and observant individuals who attended synagogue services on a regular basis. Later generations of American Jews tended to become more lax in their religious observance, however, and much less regular in their synagogue attendance. This meant that by midcentury many congregations—despite expanding membership rolls and huge throngs of worshipers on special occasions such as the High Holidays of Rosh Hashanah and Yom Kippur—found themselves welcoming only moderate gatherings on most Sabbaths and for lesser religious festivals. This pattern of attendance led congregations of the postwar era to look for ways to create some sort of flexibility in the space reserved for worship in the modern synagogue buildings they were erecting in the suburbs. They wanted to establish sanctuaries that would feel comfortable for small groups of worshipers on most occasions but that could be expanded to accommodate larger crowds when necessary.

Since World War II the most common solution to the problem of creating flexible space in American synagogues has been to design buildings in which the assembly hall and the social hall are adjacent, and divided only by a movable partition. As more and more families joined congregations for the communal activities they supported rather than for the religious experiences they provided, synagogue social halls were in any case becoming increasingly spacious and elaborate. Many were equipped with sound systems, stages, and adjoining kitchen facilities. By placing these newly important social halls next to the main sanctuaries, synagogue designers were not only recognizing the centrality of social life for their congregations but also addressing the new realities of synagogue attendance. By means of the movable partition, the worship space could be limited in size during most of the year but enlarged tremendously for particular events such as High Holiday services.

Indeed, the strikingly new exterior appearance of most American synagogues in the postwar era owes as much to the reconfiguration of sanctuaries and social halls as it does to the development of new aesthetic principles. In the design of most prewar synagogues, the principal feature of the facade was generally the building's main entrance. It was often approached by a set of stairs leading into a vestibule, which in turn allowed access to the rear of the main sanctuary. In

Figure 60. House of Israel, Carter Avenue, Ashland. This simple building housed Ashland's Orthodox congregation from 1947 to 1976. The round window above the doorway was originally adorned with a Star of David in stained glass.

Figure 61. Keneseth Israel, Taylorsville Road, Louisville. The main part of this build-ing was completed in 1964, but the sanctuary was not added until 1971.

this classic prewar design the seating in the sanctuary faced away from the main street on which the synagogue was situated. The new floor plan so often employed in postwar American synagogues forced the abandonment of this arrangement. In order to accommodate the place-ment of the social hall side by side with the assembly hall, synagogues had to be built with some feature other than the entrance to the sanctuary as the main element facing the street. Consequently, at the front of the building the new designs placed either a doorless and often windowless wall (the ark wall of the sanctuary) or the entrance to a prominent lobby allowing access to the social hall as well as the assem-bly hall, which stood side by side behind the lobby. The seating in the sanctuary would then be oriented either facing the main street on which the synagogue stood or parallel to it.

In Kentucky, all but one of the synagogue buildings erected since World War II are based on a design incorporating movable partitions between sanctuary and social hall, and none of these buildings has a vestibule at the rear of its main assembly hall. The sole exception is the tiny and featureless House of Israel synagogue in Ashland, completed in 1947 (Figure 60). The Keneseth Israel synagogue in Louisville has a uniquely curved seating arrangement that allows its splendid windows to dominate the street elevation (Figure 61), but each of Kentucky's other post-1950 synagogues features either a doorless ark-wall facade (the Adath Jeshurun building shown in Figure 62 provides an example), or a lobby-dominated front elevation (as in the Anshei Sfard building

Figure 62. Adath Jeshurun, Woodbourne Avenue, Louisville. This photograph was taken just after the synagogue was completed in 1957. From the Picture Collection of the American Jewish Archives, Cincinnati.

Figure 63. Anshei Sfard, Dutchmans Lane, Louisville. The prominent lobby of this synagogue allows direct access to both its sanctuary and its social hall.

Figure 64. The Temple, Brownsboro Road, Louisville. This building was erected in 1980, after the Adath Israel and Brith Sholom congregations consolidated to form a new assembly.

Figure 65. Ohavay Zion, Edgewater Court, Lexington. This suburban building replaced the congregation's downtown synagogue in 1986.

shown in Figure 63). The Temple in Louisville and Ohavay Zion in Lexington, both of which occupy corner lots, present an ark-wall facade to one of the streets on which they stand and a lobby entrance to the other (see Figures 64 and 65). At The Temple, the influence of attendance patterns can be seen not only in the shape of the synagogue but also in the layout of the parking lot. The Temple has provided a limited number of blacktopped spaces sufficient for the parking needs of most occasions, and it has supplemented these spaces with several grassy strips designated as areas for additional parking.

The same kinds of changing behaviors that helped bring about alterations in the overall design and outward appearance of American synagogues in the decades since World War II have also influenced the arrangement of the space within the sanctuaries of these buildings. As most American Jews of the second generation and beyond became less committed to Jewish practice, less familiar with the Hebrew languages and with religious rituals, and less regular in their attendance at synagogue services, the proportion of Jews who were comfortable as active participants in a worship service naturally declined. Reform Judaism had long acknowledged this development by transforming the liturgy and by entrusting much of it to clergymen and to choirs, sometimes made up of non-Jewish choristers who were not a part of the body of worshipers at all.

As the twentieth century progressed, however, worshipers in more traditional congregations as well were finding themselves increasingly in the role of observers rather than active participants in religious services, with rabbis and cantors beginning to function not only as prayer leaders but as surrogates for their congregants. Because of this development, it has become increasingly uncommon for the assembly halls of synagogues to be designed in the traditional manner, with a central reader's table facing the ark containing the Torah scrolls. Since World War II the less intimate auditorium style of seating has come to dominate the interior arrangement of American synagogues, especially in regions where the Jewish community has lacked a significant Orthodox component.

Indeed, many modern synagogue prayer halls have come to resemble theaters, with features such as a *bimah* set high above floor level, raked seating, carefully planned lines of sight and acoustics, lighting concentrated on the pulpit, and ark decorations that are often fine artistic creations but have about them the feeling of stage sets (see, for example, Figures 66 and 67). In Kentucky, several sanctuaries built since World War II have been designed with doorways leading directly to the *bimah,* so that the principals involved in a service can appear before the congregation without having to pass through the body of congregants. At The Temple in Louisville, even the synagogue's auxiliary chapel is equipped with a hidden circular stairway that allows

Figure 66. The interior of Adath Jeshurun's main sanctuary on Woodbourne Avenue in Louisville.

Figure 67. The main sanctuary of The Temple on Brownsboro Road in Louisville.

Figure 68. The interior of Anshei Sfard on Dutchmans Lane in Louisville. The divider at right, separating the men's and women's sections of the sanctuary, and the forward-facing reader's table are typical of Orthodox synagogues.

officiants to come through the building's equipment room and emerge on the *bimah* without being seen in the hall. Of course, the more synagogue sanctuaries are constructed to take into account the dependence of congregants on their surrogates, the more the perception is reinforced that congregants are at least to some extent spectators rather than full participants. Again, the design of a synagogue both reflects and conditions the nature of the worship service that takes place within it.

In the eight synagogues raised in Kentucky during the second half of the twentieth century, no sanctuary has been designed with a centrally placed *bimah*. Moreover, only the Orthodox Anshei Sfard synagogue in Louisville (Figure 68) was constructed with the main reader's table facing the ark, although the Keneseth Israel Synagogue in Louisville and the Ohavay Zion synagogue in Lexington have tried to maintained something of a traditional sanctuary's layout by employing curved or angled seating arrangements and by providing for a secondary reader's table facing forward. At Keneseth Israel, where the sanctuary was built with a high and relatively inaccessible *bimah*, the forward facing reader's table is situated on a makeshift platform at ground level (Figure 69). At Ohavay Zion, a small reader's stand facing the ark stands between two larger lecterns facing the congregation (Figure 70).

The departure from traditional interior design in Kentucky synagogues is also reflected in the virtual disappearance of gender-segre-

Figure 69. The interior of Keneseth Israel, Louisville, as it appeared in the early 1990s.

Figure 70. The interior of Lexington's Ohavay Zion, Edgewater Court. From the Ohavay Zion 75th anniversary booklet (1989).

gated seating. As the proportion of Kentucky Jews adhering to traditional religious practice has declined, and as the perception of women's roles in the worship service has been altered, mixed seating has become the norm for the commonwealth's congregations. This is not to say that the departure from traditional practice was always accomplished without controversy. At Louisville's Keneseth Israel, for example, the transition from separate seating to mixed seating, undertaken in 1952, was an extremely rancorous affair. A decision in favor of mixed seating was reached only after two years of upheaval that witnessed demonstrations requiring the intervention of the police, a lawsuit filed against the congregation by one of its members, the resignation of several prominent families, and the departure of the congregation's rabbi.

Separate seating for men and women remains today only in the small Beth Israel *shtible* (where what was once the dining room of the house occupied by the congregation serves as the women's section of the worship space) and in the Anshei Sfard synagogue. Moreover, at Anshei Sfard the women's section has been placed side by side with the men's section, and the partition between them (the *mechitza*) has been positioned at the center of the sanctuary and kept quite low. At Keneseth Israel, cloth hangings on the backs of the two pews at the right and left front of the sanctuary provide evidence of how the congregation once maintained a symbolic remnant of separate seating by reserving one of these pews exclusively for men and the other exclusively for women.

Changing patterns of synagogue attendance and changing levels of adherence to traditional practice have influenced the design of postwar synagogues in America in another way as well: they have created an enormous need for synagogue school facilities. Until the immediate prewar period, it was the role of synagogues as places of worship that had been emphasized. In the nineteenth and early twentieth centuries, religious education was considered either a relatively minor congregational responsibility or a task to be left for the most part to extracongregational bodies. This meant that any school facilities included in prewar synagogues were only a sort of afterthought. In Kentucky as elsewhere, congregations often relied on classrooms in outbuildings (as at the 1919 Adath Jeshurun in Louisville) or in basements (as at the 1939 Temple of Israel in Covington). If classroom wings or buildings were added to prewar synagogues, as they were at Ohavay Zion on Maxwell Street in Lexington, for example, and at Adath Israel on Third Street in Louisville, these were generally erected only after World War II. Some small synagogues, such as those in Owensboro and Henderson, never had classroom facilities at all.

By the 1950s, however, when so many American Jews of the interwar generation had lost their familiarity with Jewish observance and had abandoned regular synagogue attendance, congregations were recognizing an increasing need to teach children about the religious tradi-

Figure 71. The J.J. Gittleman Education Center at Adath Jeshurun, Louisville, named for one of the congregation's rabbis and dedicated in 1966. The incorporation of expansive classroom facilities in contemporary synagogues suggests the importance attached to education by congregations in the era after World War II.

tions and sacred texts that had become alien to their parents. As a result, most congregations made their instructional activities more central to their missions, and when they built their new suburban synagogues, these buildings became as important for their educational functions as for their social and liturgical roles. The fact that young families in the midst of a baby boom made up such a large part of congregational membership in the postwar era only enhanced the importance of education as a synagogue responsibility. Consequently, the contemporary synagogues of Kentucky, like nearly all postwar synagogues throughout the country, were planned with classroom facilities as integral elements in their design. When Adath Jeshurun erected its building in Louisville's Highlands, for example, the architectural scheme integrated the mansion that was on the site for temporary use as a school (the house was screened by a garden wall to reduce its visibility) and provided for the addition of a classroom wing when money became available (see Figure 71). And, as we have seen, both the Anshei Sfard and Keneseth Israel congregations erected school facilities at their new suburban locations in Louisville several years before they even broke ground for their main sanctuaries.

The integration of school facilities and the introduction of larger and more elaborate social halls into the designs of postwar synagogues are clear indications that by the second half of the twentieth century,

Figure 72. The small chapel installed at Adath Jeshurun in 1957 as it appeared in the early 1990s. A complete renovation in 1994 made the chapel more comfortable and more intimate and reflects a recent trend among American congregations to create worship spaces that foster a greater sense of warmth and participation in prayer.

synagogues were being expected to fulfill a multiplicity of functions. Because of their expanding roles, synagogues (by now often referred to as "synagogue centers" in some parts of the country) had to be environments in which an increasingly professionalized staff could operate smoothly and efficiently. Thus the expansive synagogue buildings of the postwar era have typically included not only assembly halls, social halls, and classrooms but also spacious reception areas, administrative offices of various sorts, and comfortably furnished studies for the rabbis. Libraries, youth lounges, and gift shops as well have become standard features in all but the smallest of America's synagogues (in a modest building such as Temple Israel in Paducah, a set of bookshelves may serve as a library, and a glass display case may take the place of a gift shop). Auxiliary chapels used for small-scale functions such as weekday services are another important feature of contemporary synagogue buildings, although these were common in the larger synagogues of the pre–World War II era as well (see Figure 72 for an example).

Even though Kentucky's newest synagogue buildings have been heavily influenced by postwar trends in architectural design and have been erected in conformity with several practical considerations, it should not be assumed that they, or synagogues elsewhere in America, have lost all connection with their architectural past. Many congregations have taken care to preserve some evidence of their prewar architectural heritage in their new houses of prayer and have sought to hark

Figure 73. The rear of the main sanctuary at Keneseth Israel, Louisville, featuring colored glass windows with holiday motifs.

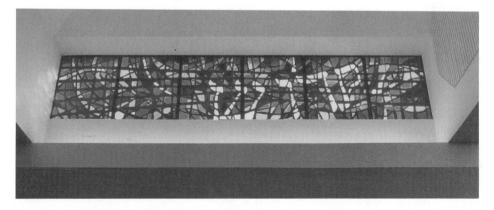

Figure 74. A faceted glass window from The Temple in Louisville, incorporating the word *kadosh*, meaning "holy."

back to old associations even as they constructed buildings with radically new designs. For example, several contemporary Kentucky synagogues have made prominent use of artistically designed windows, an element long associated with American synagogue architecture. Examples of colored glass artistry can be seen in the windows by William L. Fischer at Louisville's Keneseth Israel synagogue, by Robert Markert at The Temple, and by Guy Kemper at Ohavay Zion in Lexington (see Figures 73, 74, and 70).

Figure 75. The tablets of the Ten Commandments from the Brith Sholom building on Second Street at College in Louisville. They are now installed in the interior courtyard at The Temple.

Some late twentieth-century congregations, like those at the turn of the century, have also tried to build Near Eastern associations into their synagogues in order to evoke the fundamental connection of the Jewish people with the Land of Israel. The new Ohavay Zion building in Lexington, for instance, has a lobby floor of imported Jerusalem marble, and at the 1989 Temple Shalom in Louisville both the arched roof and the exterior blocks are intended to echo the forms and hues of the Holy City, if only faintly.[5] If anything, the nostalgia of American congregations for their architectural past is growing as the twenty-first century approaches, and some are seeking to recover lost synagogue artifacts. When Adath Jeshurun recovered the tablets of the Ten Commandments that had once flanked the ark of its domed downtown sanctuary, it gave them a place of honor in the lobby of its current building, and at The Temple the Ten Commandments from the old downtown sanctuary of Brith Sholom on Second Street are on display in a courtyard (see Figure 75).

Just as it is difficult to know how most of Kentucky's congregations of the nineteenth and early twentieth centuries selected the architects to design their buildings, it is also hard to discover exactly how local congregations went about choosing their architects in more recent decades. Much of the discussion of this issue must have gone on informally, and many of the considerations involved were left unrecorded. The question of selection of architects and congregational interaction with these professionals remains a significant one, given the extent to which synagogue buildings are reflections of the assemblies they house. The art historian Avram Kampf has commented on the potentially problematic position of post–World War II synagogue architects or artists who work for congregations on a "strictly contractual" basis, without being privy to their inner dynamics; and the interior designer Efrem Weitzman, who created the ark and its accessories for The Temple in Louisville, has pointed out that the relationship between the various individuals and groups that have a part in the design of a synagogue is seldom without some strains.[6] But little historical research has been done on the commissioning of synagogue architects, and this makes an assessment of the relationship between Kentucky congregations and their architects especially important.[7] It is certainly possible that the patterns observable in Kentucky have been duplicated elsewhere in America and beyond.

One thing that can be said is that at least since the end of World War I, Kentucky congregations have shown a decided preference for employing Jewish architects, or at least architectural firms with Jewish partners. None of the professionals known to have designed a Kentucky synagogue before the end of World War I was Jewish, but it appears that even as early as 1904, Louisville's Adath Israel was already showing something of a bias in favor of Jewish architects. Although the commission for Adath Israel was eventually awarded to McDonald and Sheblessy, when the congregation first solicited proposals for its new temple, most of the out-of-town architects it approached were Jews. Among these were Albert Kahn of Detroit, Leon Stern of Rochester, and A.F. Rosenheim of Los Angeles.[8]

In the interwar period, Jewish architects came to predominate as synagogue designers in Kentucky. Leon Frankel designed Lexington's Adath Israel; the firm of Joseph and Joseph was responsible for Louisville's Keneseth Israel; and Leslie Moss planned Covington's Temple of Israel. Of the eight synagogues built in Kentucky since 1950, five were designed by architectural firms in which some or all of the partners were Jews. In addition, the main sanctuary and auditorium additions of the Keneseth Israel building on Taylorsville Road were designed by Jewish firms, even though the original synagogue building of 1964 was planned by Thomas Nolan and Sons, a firm without Jewish connections.

There are several reasons why congregations may have begun looking to Jewish firms as the twentieth century progressed. Building committees may have thought that Jewish architects would be more aware of recent trends in synagogue construction and more sensitive to the ongoing issue of finding a suitable style for American synagogues. Indeed, in the 1950s the most important commentator on American synagogue architecture of her day, Rachel Wischnitzer, asserted that the appearance of an increasing number of Jewish architects in America would finally bring a solution to the enigma of how a synagogue should look.[9] In this regard, it is worth noting that the only postwar Kentucky synagogue built in a revival style, the Brith Sholom building put up in the mid-1950s, was designed by the architectural partnership of Walter C. Wagner and Joseph Potts, neither of whom was a Jew.

Perhaps congregational building committees favored Jewish architects also because they felt that Jews would bring to their work a greater familiarity with Jewish practices, that they would already be aware of such design issues as the placement of the *bimah* and gender-specific seating. Although this supposition may have been valid to some extent, it should not be assumed that the Jewish architects who built synagogues in Kentucky were particularly observant or Jewishly knowledgeable individuals. Even those commissioned by Kentucky's Orthodox congregations were not themselves traditional in practice or belief. Leslie Moss, who built the 1939 Temple of Israel, does not seem to have identified strongly with his faith at all; it appears that at least two of his children married non-Jews in an era when that was still very uncommon, and when Moss himself died in 1966, he was unaffiliated with any Jewish congregation or organization.[10] So too, the partners in the Joseph family firm that built Keneseth Israel's 1929 synagogue, the main sanctuary for its 1964 building, and also the Anshei Sfard synagogue, were themselves members of the Reform congregation Adath Israel.

Another reason that Jewish architects may have been chosen to design so many of Kentucky's synagogues since the 1920s is that they had preexisting contacts within the Jewish community. It may simply have been considered good form to do business with individuals who were already known in the community and who were likely to be actively involved and committed to it. There may even have been a feeling that employing members of the local Jewish community would have some financial benefits: perhaps they would be inclined to charge lower fees.

Of course, all these considerations were even more compelling when a congregation that was contemplating the construction of a new house of worship had architects among its own members. Lexington's Adath Israel probably felt that it had no choice but to invite Leon Frankel to design its new building in the 1920s, for besides being one of Lexington's premier architects, Frankel was an active member of the congregation. He was on the board of directors of Adath Israel for some twenty-five years and even served as president of the congregation from 1930 to 1932.[11]

When Louisville's Adath Israel began working on plans for a new synagogue in 1976, even before it merged with Brith Sholom to create The Temple, it set up interviews with at least half a dozen architects, including the designer of the Isaac M. Wise Temple that had just been erected in Cincinnati. Within a few weeks, however, Adath Israel abandoned its consultations with all other firms and concluded an arrangement whereby the competing Louisville firms of Arrasmith Judd Rapp, and Joseph and Joseph would undertake the erection of a new building as a joint venture.[12] This happened because in Arnold Judd and Alfred Joseph, Jr., both of these firms had senior partners who were members of Adath Israel. Even though the principal design architect for The Temple turned out to be John Chovan of Arrasmith Judd Rapp, a non-Jew, both Judd and Joseph remained intimately involved with the construction of the building, and it was clearly their presence in the congregation that had driven the selection of their firms for the project.

Communal and congregational connections also help explain the selection of building contractors for several synagogues. Among the construction companies owned by Jews that have been involved in the building of Kentucky synagogues over the years are the Shilmeister firm of Covington, the Platoff and Bush firm of Louisville, and the Ale Bornstein firm, also of Louisville.

It appears that the inclination of Kentucky congregations to turn to Jewish architectural firms was reinforced in several cases by the fact that these firms had had previous experience in designing projects for Jewish institutions. Joseph and Joseph no doubt benefited in the post–World War II era from the part one of its founders had played in the design of the Adath Israel building on Third Street and the firm's construction of the Keneseth Israel building at Jacob and Floyd. In the early 1950s, just before it undertook several new synagogue projects, Joseph and Joseph also won the commissions for the Standard Country Club, which serves a primarily Jewish clientele, and for Louisville's Jewish Hospital. Similarly, Gerald Baron, who designed the 1989 Temple Shalom building in Louisville, had previously won a commission for work on the Shalom Tower, a subsidized housing facility under the sponsorship of the Louisville Jewish community, and it was Baron who designed the 1982 addition to the Keneseth Israel synagogue on Taylorsville Road.

Indeed, extensive experience in working with Jewish organizations seems to have been the one factor whereby an outsider could lure Kentucky congregations away from local architects. Of all the architectural firms known to have been employed in the construction of Kentucky synagogues since the 1920s, only two were not local concerns, and both had a history of substantial commissions from Jewish institutions. The two out-of-town firms that built synagogues in Kentucky were Braverman and Halperin of Cleveland, which designed the 1957 Adath Jeshurun synagogue in Louisville; and Pepinsky, Grau, Shroud, and Shorr of Cincinnati, which designed the 1963 Temple Israel building in Paducah.

The members of Adath Jeshurun's building committee in the early 1950s made it clear that the matter of prior experience weighed heavily in their deliberations as they searched for an architect. In 1954, announcing the selection of the firm of Sigmund Braverman and M.P. Halperin, the committee observed that "the choice of an architect is of the utmost importance for any building program, but more so for a synagogue, which requires a thorough knowledge of synagogue tradition. . . . In these days of high construction costs, it requires long experience to be able to exercise the maximum economy without sacrificing the inspiration of synagogue art."[13] The committee was no doubt impressed by the fact that Braverman and Halperin had already designed more than twenty synagogues in the United States and Canada. Among the buildings conceived by the Hungarian-born Braverman, who became the principal architect for the Adath Jeshurun project, were the Beth El synagogue in Akron, Temple Israel in Canton, Temple Emanu El in Cleveland, and Temple Israel in Omaha. Members of the Adath Jeshurun building committee had made inspection trips to Akron, Canton, and Cleveland.

Still, even after Adath Jeshurun selected Braverman and Halperin, there remained a desire and probably a need for local involvement. Although the congregation had rejected an architectural plan submitted by Joseph and Joseph by a vote of twelve to eight, it appointed that firm as "supervising architects" to work with Braverman. And when the time came to add an education building to the Adath Jeshurun synagogue, Joseph and Joseph did that project on its own (the firm of the Jewish architect Arnold Judd had also presented a plan for this project, but it was not accepted).

Information is not available to explain how the Temple Israel congregation of Paducah chose Pepinsky, Grau, Shroud, and Shorr to build its 1963 synagogue, but it is known that shortly before Bernard Pepinsky's firm was commissioned, it had finished work on the Jewish Community Center of Cincinnati. Pepinsky himself had been an honorary president of the center since 1955, and he was also active in the regional Council of Jewish Federations and Welfare Funds.

In general, then, it seems that since quite early in the twentieth century, Kentucky congregations have considered the ideal designer for a synagogue to be a Jewish architect with a local firm. In the only cases where local Jewish architectural firms were not employed, two congregations opted for Jewish firms from out of town, and three opted for local firms not directed by Jews. It is not clear why Louisville's Brith Sholom chose Wagner and Potts as the architects for its temple on Cowling Avenue, but it seems that Keneseth Israel chose Thomas Nolan and Sons to build the first part of its complex on Taylorsville Road simply because the congregation had once gotten advice about structural problems at its downtown synagogue from the founder of that firm.[14] It may also have been significant that both Walter Wagner of Wagner and Potts and Robert Nolan of Nolan and Sons had extensive experience in ecclesiastical architecture as designers of several Catholic churches in Louisville.

According to Steve Caller, co-chairman of the building committee that oversaw construction of Lexington's new Ohavay Zion synagogue, his congregation had very specific reasons for employing the local architectural partnership of Pearson, Bender and Jolly: it was selected because of the "youth, enthusiasm and obvious interest" of the three University of Kentucky architecture graduates who had recently established the firm. Although all three were non-Jews, they promised to give the Ohavay Zion project "special attention," and at least one partner (Charles Jolly) spent a lot of time attending services, studying Jewish holidays, and getting to know the congregation's habits.[15]

Of course, even fuller information about how Kentucky's synagogue architects were selected would still leave open the question of how much control congregations retained over the final appearance of their buildings. In a sense, the fundamental arbiters of how their houses of worship would look were congregations themselves, for it was they who—either directly or through their representatives—reviewed plans and selected architects. No congregation would choose an architect whose proposal did not reflect its own vision of how its synagogue should look. Moreover, by regulating the amount of funding available for construction, a congregation imposed a great deal of control over the ultimate appearance of its synagogue. Robert Nolan, Sr., the designer of the 1964 Keneseth Israel building in Louisville, has said that he would have built a more monumental structure had his budget allowed, and Gerald Baron has also commented that financial limitations dictated many of his decisions about the building he designed for Temple Shalom.[16] Cost consciousness affected the design even of The Temple, a building that cost some $4 million to construct in 1980. In order to save money, The Temple was erected without a separate boardroom, for example, and with low-quality exterior doors that soon had to be replaced.[17]

Anecdotal and, in a few cases, documentary evidence suggests that throughout the twentieth century most architects commissioned to build synagogues in Kentucky were given a relatively free hand once they were engaged. Nonetheless, in each congregation that initiated a construction project there were usually a few centrally involved people who worked closely with the architect, representing what they saw as the congregation's needs and best interests. Often these individuals were members of the synagogue's building committee. For example, Richard Wolf of The Temple's building committee reports that he and his co-chair, Alvin Rouben, resolved to "run the project" themselves in order to keep it moving. They would consult with committees, with the congregation's rabbis, and with the architects involved in design, but once a decision had been made on a particular issue (how big the gift shop should be, or where bathrooms should be located, or whether or not the choir should be visible during services), they were determined that the matter would be closed. On several occasions, Wolf and Rouben had to threaten to resign their positions in order to maintain their vision of how the construction process should proceed. Similarly, Steve Caller of Lexington's Ohavay Zion relates that his building committee of three "key people" had "a heavy hand in the overall design," doing "90 percent of the design coordination [and] material selections."[18]

The extensive manuscript records that have survived relating to the construction of Adath Israel's 1906 temple suggest that the same kind of continuous involvement by a congregational building committee could be found early in the century as well. The Adath Israel committee had a say even in such seemingly trivial matters as what kind of track to use for folding partitions between rooms, and whether or not to run the temple's electric wires through steel tubing.[19]

In the construction of Adath Jeshurun's 1919 building too there seems to have been some input from the congregation's representatives and even some disagreements with the architect. It appears, for example, that the congregation rejected James Gaffney's choice of a light-colored paint for the interior of the dome, and selected a darker tint. The result was a synagogue that some considered too dimly lit, and in 1922 a proposal was made to suspend a lighting fixture from the center of the dome. The plan was never put into effect, however, as Gaffney's firm advised the congregation that the dome was never designed to carry such an added weight and that "from the standpoint of architectural design we do not believe that it would help the looks of the interior of the Temple."[20]

When Adath Jeshurun built its new synagogue in the Highlands, members of the building committee again played an active role and again found themselves in disagreement with their architect at times. The committee rejected several early designs submitted by Braverman and Halperin before settling on what was called "plan K," and they carried on extensive correspondence with their architect on matters such as what color of floor tiles and carpets should be selected, what kinds of seats and lecterns should be purchased, what kitchen equipment should be installed, and where plaques acknowledging contributions should be placed.

Certainly the greatest disagreement concerned the sculpture that Sigmund Braverman commissioned Cleveland artist Henry Roth to create for the front of the Adath Jeshurun synagogue (Figure 76). As soon as the sculpture was installed, around September of 1957, congregants began to express their dismay; they could not understand what the piece was intended to represent, and they did not like it. In October

Figure 76. The controversial sculpture by Henry Roth on the facade of the 1957 Adath Jeshurun synagogue in Louisville.

the president of Adath Jeshurun, Bernard Goldstein, wrote to Braverman: "The Congregation is very unhappy [with the Roth sculpture] and has directed that it be removed." Characterizing the piece as "completely abstract and unrecognizable modern art," Goldstein argued that it was nothing like what the congregation had been told to expect. He demanded "full credit for [its] cost" and requested that Braverman arrange to take down the sculpture as soon as possible. "Since the feeling against it is so strong," Goldstein observed, "it would jeopardize the continued harmony in our Congregation to let it remain any longer."

In the face of all this opposition, Braverman attempted to vindicate his commissioning of the Roth sculpture. Describing the piece as "a stylized menorah, one of the few authentic symbols [of Judaism], resting on two elements which can be interpreted as two wings of the cherubin [*sic*] enclosing a burning bush motif," he explained his decision to install an "avant-garde" sculpture by arguing that "living Judaism can only be expressed by living art." Henry Roth addressed the congregation on the matter of his controversial creation as well. In a rather pointed and condescending note he declared, "In the sculpture for the Adath Jeshurun Synagogue, I have tried to create a beautiful and expressive linear form." He complained that "the layman expects a literal representation of everything. . . . If he cannot recognize some symbol in a form, he ridicules it. Usually, he simply does not understand the purpose of art."

As part of his campaign to defend his choice of artwork, Braverman even dispatched William McVeigh, then head of the Cleveland Institute of Art, to render his opinion. After visiting Louisville, McVeigh pronounced the Roth work "aesthetically sound . . . [and] among the upper third of all acceptable pieces in the country." That might be "the professional view of it," building committee chairman Robert Berman responded, but "the trouble is, the people in our congregation are not professional [art critics]." The debate over the Roth sculpture and the resulting debate over Braverman's fee continued well into 1959, but eventually tempers must have cooled. Despite all the turmoil that surrounded the installation of the Adath Jeshurun sculpture, Braverman's bill was settled in September 1959, and Roth's creation remains in place to this day.[21]

Sometimes it was the rabbi, rather than lay leaders, who took on the task of representing a congregation's interests in the course of a building program. When Adath Israel installed the magnificent stained glass windows in its Third Street temple, for example, the main link between the congregation and the artist, Harry Eldredge Goodhue of Cambridge, Massachusetts, was Adath Israel's rabbi at the time, H.G. Enelow. Rabbi Enelow monitored work on the windows very carefully, commenting on each window in great detail. "For the figure of the Prophet . . . you might introduce an entirely different countenance," he suggested in one letter to Goodhue. "You could also add in the background of the lunette a suggestion of the vine and the fig tree, symbols of peace," he wrote in another. Enelow consulted on the verses that would be inscribed in the windows ("I suggest the Hebrew verse Jeremiah 24:7, for the border") and he even dealt with technical matters of installation ("The window was unpacked this morning, and I regret to have to write you that one piece was found in broken condition").[22]

Another example of rabbinic involvement comes from the story of the construction of the Anshei Sfard synagogue in the early 1960s. It appears that as the sanctuary was being designed, it was Rabbi Solomon Roodman, spiritual leader of the congregation since just after World War II, who suggested the *bimah* arrangement to be used in the assembly hall. It was also Rabbi Roodman who, knowing the demographic characteristics and the habits of his congregants, advocated the creation of a relatively small worship space so that it would not seem empty during normal Sabbath services.[23]

In the end, then, the synagogues of Kentucky have been fashioned by many different forces. These buildings have given substance to the visions of various rabbis and congregational leaders, and they have

Figure 77. The Temple of Israel building in Covington as it looked in the early 1990s. The roof line has been changed completely, and little evidence remains that it was once a synagogue (compare Figure 41).

embodied the creative talents of the architects who oversaw their design or renovation. Their character also has been influenced by the multifaceted tradition of synagogue architecture in America, and the historical development of American Judaism itself has helped to shape their appearance. Of course, as congregational response to the Roth sculpture at Adath Jeshurun suggests, individuals did not always react to buildings the way those who conceived them intended. In recent years, literary criticism has emphasized the idea that every reader can impart his or her own meaning to a written text, perhaps a meaning very different from the one the writer had in mind. In the same way, it is important to appreciate that buildings can be understood in a multiplicity of ways by their creators and by the various people who encounter them. Nonetheless, whether they were erected as Jewish houses of worship or converted from other uses, all of Kentucky's synagogues have reflected both the philosophical and the practical concerns of the congregations they served, and all have said something about the resources available to those congregations. In a theoretical sense, then, these buildings can be "deconstructed" to reveal a great deal about the people who built and used them, and hence about Jewish life in the commonwealth more generally.

Because Kentucky's synagogues can tell us so much about Jewish life at the local level, and because they bear witness to the commonwealth's diverse and fascinating architectural heritage, the fate of these houses of worship should be of great concern. As the twenty-first century approaches, over one third of the buildings that have served as synagogues in the commonwealth are no longer standing. Among these, nine were constructed specifically as Jewish houses of prayer. Moreover, synagogue buildings in towns such as Henderson, Ashland, and Covington are no longer serving Jewish congregations, and these structures face an uncertain future (see, for example, Figure 77). There is special reason to be concerned about the fate of the former Adas Israel building in Henderson and of the Adath Israel temple in Owensboro, sustained now by only a handful of individuals. Both meetinghouses are rare examples of surviving nineteenth-century synagogues, of which only about four dozen are extant in the entire United States.[24]

As Kentucky enters its third century of statehood, the value of the former synagogues that are still standing in the commonwealth must come to be more completely appreciated, and the significance of the buildings that are currently serving Kentucky's Jewish congregations must come to be recognized more widely. Perhaps this book will stimulate a heightened interest in those synagogue buildings around the state that can still be visited and explored, even as it serves to perpetuate the memory of those Kentucky synagogues that have already vanished.

Discovering Kentucky's Synagogues

An Essay on Bibliography
and Methodology

Discovering Kentucky's Synagogues

An Essay on Bibliography and Methodology

THE AVAILABLE SOURCES of information about Kentucky's congregations and synagogue buildings are widely scattered and highly varied, and in order to compile the information and create the visual record presented in this book, it was necessary to gather bits of data and individual images from a great many places. This essay reviews the many sources I used and examines some of the research problems I encountered. For researchers who may want to consult this volume as a model for synagogue surveys in other regions of the United States, this essay will be especially useful for what it reveals about research methodology. For readers seeking an introduction to the larger sweep of Kentucky's Jewish history, it can function as a guide to much of the literature available about Jewish life in the Bluegrass State.

Perhaps because Kentucky has always had such a small Jewish population, very little scholarly research has been done on the history of Jews in the commonwealth, but a few journalists and amateur historians have produced a variety of very useful reports. These accounts, usually dealing with individual congregations or individual Jewish communities, vary widely in their depth of coverage and in their accuracy, but wherever they exist, they were among the first sources I consulted as I approached the task of compiling accurate data on all of Kentucky's congregations and synagogue buildings.

Nearly half of the state's synagogues have been located in the city of Louisville, and, fortunately there is a very valuable narrative available about developments in the commonwealth's most important center of Jewish life. This is Herman Landau's book *Adath Louisville: The Story of a Jewish Community* (Louisville, 1981), which contains historical data and informative anecdotes about all of Louisville's Jewish congregations except the second Beth Israel and Adat B'nai Yisrael, which had not yet been established when the book was written. Helpful for learning about some of Louisville individual congregations were the brief histories produced by some of the synagogues themselves. Keneseth Israel included a historical sketch in the booklet it issued when its present sanctuary was dedicated in 1971, and Anshei Sfard incorporated a historical review in its eightieth anniversary booklet of 1973.

Newspaper and magazine articles are essential sources of information for any study of local Jewish history, and I relied on many periodicals. Although the Louisville Free Public Library has a manuscript index going back to 1917 for the city's most important newspaper, the *Louisville Courier-Journal*, locating all the newspaper and magazine stories that have dealt with the various congregations and synagogues of Kentucky's largest city was still a very difficult task. In addition to items traced through the library's index, I discovered others as clippings preserved in archival collections. The following articles are representative of those published over the years relating to Louisville's synagogues: "Temple Adath Israel to Celebrate Anniversary," *Courier-Journal*, January 12, 1918; "Knesseth Israel [*sic*] Buys Site for Synagogue," *Courier-Journal,* December 16, 1927; "Adath Jeshurun Starts Fund Drive for New Synagogue in Highlands," *Louisville Times*, August 21, 1953; "New Building Opened by Keneseth Israel," *Courier-Journal*, December 7, 1964; "New Congregation Leaves Merged Reform Temple," *Courier-Journal*, October 9, 1976; "Historic Buildings . . . Bonnycastle Group Wants to Sell Synagogue, Home," *Neighborhoods/East End* (weekly supplement to the *Courier-Journal*), February 6–7, 1980; "Illuminating Jewish Holidays" (an article by Marshall and Jane Portnoy about the colored glass windows at the Keneseth Israel synagogue), *Louisville* magazine, September 1983; and "Temple Shalom Realizes Dream of Own Synagogue," *Neighborhoods/East End*, August 30, 1989.

Sources I consulted in researching Jewish congregations and synagogues in Lexington include the congregational history of Ohavay Zion published in its sisterhood yearbook of 1959, and the historical review published in the synagogue's seventy-fifth anniversary booklet of 1989.

Also important for Lexington are the Adath Israel history appearing in the program for the 1926 dedication of its Ashland Avenue temple and the histories contained in the congregation's seventy-fifth and eighty-fifth anniversary booklets, published in 1979 and 1988, respectively.

Information about Jewish congregational life in Paducah appears in several newspaper stories published since the 1960s. The most important of these are "Rabbi Max Kaufman Has Served Here 17 Years," *Paducah Sun-Democrat*, May 22, 1966; and "Looking Back: 100th Anniversary Time of Reflection for Paducah Jews," *Paducah Sun*, May 6, 1979. Some helpful references to the Jewish community can also be gleaned from Fred G. Neuman's *The Story of Paducah* (Paducah, Ky. [?], 1927; revised edition 1979); and from Camille Wells's *Architecture of Paducah and McCracken County* (Paducah, Ky., 1981).

Two newspaper articles in the *Owensboro Messenger-Inquirer* that proved helpful for learning about the congregation and synagogue in Owensboro are "A Matter of Faith: Jewish Community Faces Uncertain Future," December 1, 1983; and Beth Wilson's "Building upon a Belief: History of Judaism, Local Temple Told," February 11, 1985. I also consulted William Foster Hayes's *Sixty Years of Owensboro, 1883–1943* (Owensboro, Ky., c. 1943), and *Historical Churches of Daviess County* (Owensboro, Ky., 1976).

On the Henderson congregation, there is Spalding Trafton's "Laying the Cornerstone and Dedication of Temple Adas Israel 33 Years Ago," *Henderson Gleaner and Journal,* March 1, 1925; and a mention in *The History of Henderson County, Kentucky*, edited by Frieda J. Dannheiser (Evansville, Ind., 1980).

Useful information on the congregation in Hopkinsville came from a news story written by Cecil Hendron when the roof of the city's synagogue collapsed: "Rebuilding of Jewish Synagogue Is Unlikely," *Kentucky New Era*, November 7, 1977. On Hopkinsville there is also Jerry Bohn's two-page notice "America's Smallest Jewish Community," *Jewish Digest* 14 (January 1969).

The most valuable source on Jewish congregational life in Covington is Leslie A. Lassetter's 1976 research paper, "Covington's Schule, The Temple of Israel," on file at the Kenton County Public Library. In the same library's newspaper index I found several helpful items from the early twentieth century. Chief among these, all in the *Kentucky Post,* are "Hebrews Will Celebrate Arrival of Sofer Torah [*sic*]," February 16, 1907; "Hebrew Congregation Is Incorporated," December 16, 1914; and "New Jewish Temple for Covington," January 8, 1915. Also helpful on Covington are two newspaper articles by Leslie Lapides, published under the heading "Judaism Then and Now," *Kentucky Post*, March 19, 1983.

The newspaper index at the Kenton County Public Library in Covington also disclosed some important news items concerning Jewish life in neighboring Newport. These include "House of Worship" (about the incorporation of Newport's congregation), *Kentucky Post*, February 10, 1897; and "Bible Presentation" (about the dedication of the Newport synagogue), *Kentucky Post*, January 23, 1905. The Agudath Achim congregation in Ashland is mentioned briefly in *A History of Ashland, Kentucky, 1786–1954* (Ashland, Ky., 1954).

Informative as all these newspaper articles and other local sources are, however, they do not cover all of Kentucky's Jewish communities, and seldom do they provide enough detail about individual congregations or synagogues to make a complete and accurate summary of their histories possible. Moreover, most of the historical sketches and newspaper stories available were hurriedly produced by writers untrained in the discipline of history, and unmindful of the need to verify their information and to indicate the origins of their data. In fact, many accounts of Kentucky's Jewish history are heavily dependent upon the memories of individual men and women, and these memories are frequently unreliable. It was clearly impossible to depend on such accounts alone in conducting this study.

Often I derived additional information about Kentucky's Jewish congregations and their synagogues from site visits; for getting to know the history and the character of an individual building, there is really no substitute for inspecting its various spaces, reading its plaques and inscriptions, and touching its surfaces. In a few cases, local informants also supplemented what I had learned from newspapers and the other sources cited above. But again, the men and women I interviewed often admitted to lapses of memory or to uncertainty, and in any event the accuracy of personal recollections is always open to some question. Ultimately, only research in printed primary sources allowed me to fill in the gaps and check the validity of secondary sources and oral testimony.

Certainly the most valuable printed primary sources I consulted for this study were the city directories for the various Kentucky towns where Jewish communities have existed over the years. City directories have been the standard references for information about local populations in cities and towns across the United States since the early nineteenth century. Typically, these annual publications contain classified sections that provide information about goods and services; civic sections that deal with local government and community life; and alphabetical listings of individuals, businesses, and institutions, sometimes supplemented by street guides that indicate the occupants of every building in the city, house by house. Thus it is not unusual for local religious organizations, including those of the Jewish community, to appear several times in any given volume. An individual congregation might appear once in the church listings of the civic section, again in the alphabetical section under its name, and yet a third time in the

CARON'S 1892 DIRECTORY. 45

CALVARY CHURCH—913 Fourth av. Rev. J. G. Minnigerode, rector. Services at 11 a. m. and 7:30 p. m. Sunday-school at 9:30 a. m.

CHURCH OF THE ADVENT—1607 Baxter av. Communion at 7 a. m. Services at 10:30 a. m. Bible Class at 9:30 a. m. Sunday-school at 3 p. m.

ST. ANDREW'S CHURCH—1055 Second. Rev. C. C. Penick, rector. Services at 11 a. m. and 8 p. m. Sunday-school at 9:30 a. m. Services Wednesday at 8 p. m.

ST. STEPHEN'S MISSION—1803 Fischer av. Services at 11 a. m. Sunday-school at 2 p. m.

ST. PETER'S CHURCH—3412 High av. Rev. G. G. Smith, pastor. Services at 7 and 11 a. m. and 8 p. m. Sunday-school at 9:15 a. m.

CALVARY CHAPEL—111 Campbell. Rev. J. G. Minnigerode, rector. Services second Sunday in each month at 4 p, m. Sunday-school at 3 p. m.

ASCENSION MISSION—2223 W. Walnut. Rev. G. C. Waller, rector. Services at 10:45 a. m. and 8 p. m. Prayer meeting Wednesday at 7:45 p. m. Sunday-school at 9:15 a. m.

CHURCH OF OUR MERCIFUL SAVIOR (COLORED)—1031 W. Walnut. Rev. A. Brown, rector. Services at 10:30 a. m. and 7:30 p. m. Sunday-school at 9:30 a. m. and 3:30 p. m. Parochial school attached.

BROTHERHOOD OF ST. ANDREW—A layman's organization of the Episcopal Church in the United States and Canada.

LOCAL COUNCIL—Composed of two representatives from each chapter in Louisville. Meets the Second Thursday of every month at 8 p. m. 525 Second street. Officers: S. L. Fraser, President; D. W. Gray, Vice President; John W. Clarke, Secretary and Treasurer.

GERMAN EVANGELICAL.

ST. MATTHEW'S CHURCH—611 Mechanic. Rev. Otto C. Miner, pastor. Services (German), 10:15 a. m. English, 7:30 p. m. Sunday-school (German), 9:30 a. m. English, 2 p. m.

ST. PAUL'S CHURCH—Preston, northeast cor. Green. Rev. Frederick Weygold, pastor. Services (German) at 10 a. m. and 7:30 p. m. Sunday-school at 9 a. m. and 2 p. m.

ST. PETER'S CHURCH—1030 Grayson. Rev. Henry Waldmann, pastor. Services at 10 a. m. and 7 p. m. Sunday-school at 8:30 a. m. Prayer-meeting Wednesday at 7:45 p. m.

ST. JOHN'S CHURCH—651 E. Market. Rev. Carl J. Zimmermann, pastor. Services at 10:15 a. m. and 7:30 p. m. Sunday-school (German) at 9 a. m. English, 3 p. m. Prayer-meeting Wednesday at 7:30 p. m.

ST. LUCAS GERMAN EVANGELICAL CHURCH—1824 W. Jefferson. Rev. L. A. Michel, pastor. Services at 10:15 a. m. and 7:30 p. m. Sunday-school at 9 a. m. Prayer-meeting Wednesday at 7:30 p. m.

GERMAN EVANGELICAL CHRIST CHURCH—1006 Garden. Rev. A. Schory, pastor. Services at 10 a. m. and 7:30 p. m.

Sunday-school at 9 a. m. Bible class Wednesday evening at 7:30.

GERMAN EVANGELICAL BETHLEHEM CHURCH—1354 7th. Rev. O. W. Breuhaus, pastor. Services at 10 a. m. and 7 p. m. Sunday-school at 9 a. m.

(Reformed.)

GERMAN EVANGELICAL REFORMED SALEM CHURCH — 1716 Prentice. Rev. C. F. Kriete, pastor. Services at 10:30 a. m. and 7 p. m. Sunday-school at 9 a. m. Prayer-meeting Thursday at 7 p. m.

ZION CHURCH—912 Hancock. Rev. C. M. Schaaf, pastor. Services at 10 a. m. and 7 p. m. Sunday-school at 9 a. m. Prayer-meeting Thursday at 7:30 p. m.

EVANGELICAL ASSOCIATION.

NEW SALEM EVANGELICAL ASSOCIATION MISSION—Mercer, nw cor Grayson. Rev. Jacob Young, pastor. Services at 10:30 a. m. and 7:30 p. m. Sunday-school 9:15 a. m. Prayer meeting Wednesday at 7:30 p. m.

ZION'S CHURCH OF THE EVANGELICAL ASSOCIATION—910 E. Walnut. Rev. G. M. Hallwachs, pastor. Services at 10:30 a. m. and 7:30 p. m. Sunday-school at 9 a. m. Prayer meeting Tuesdays, Wednesdays and Thursdays.

ISRAEL.

TEMPLE ADAS ISRAEL—Broadway, corner Sixth. Rev. A. Moses, rabbi; N. Block, pres; J. Bamberger, vice pres; I. David, sec. Services every Friday at 8 p. m. and Saturday at 10 a. m.

SYNAGOGUE BETH ISRAEL (OLD RITUAL)—127 W. Green. Rev. L. N. Dembitz, rabbi; Abraham Steinhardt, pres; Morris Cohn, vice pres; G. S. Rosenberg, sec. Services Friday at 6 p. m. and Saturday at 8:30 a. m.

TEMPLE BRITH SHOLUM—First, between Walnut and Chestnut. Rev. Henry Kuttner, rabbi. Services Friday at 7:30 p. m. and Saturday at 10 a. m.

BNAI JAKOB CONGREGATION—454 E. Jefferson. Services daily at 7 a. m. and 6 p. m.

BETH MEDRISH HOGODEL CONGREGATION—330 E. Jefferson. Max Kabetzky, rabbi. Services every day, except Saturday, at 6 a. m. and 6 p. m. Saturday 7:30 a. m. and 4 and 6 p. m.

LUTHERAN.

FIRST ENGLISH LUTHERAN—417 E. Broadway. Rev. S. S. Waltz, pastor. Services at 11 a. m. and 7:30 p. m. Sunday-school at 9:30 a. m. Prayer meeting and lecture Wednesday at 7:30 p. m.

SECOND ENGLISH LUTHERAN—1821 W. Walnut. Rev. Harlan K. Fenner pastor. Services at 11 a. m. and 7:30 p. m. Sunday-school at 9:30 a. m. Prayer meeting Wednesday at 8 p. m.

FIRST GERMAN EVANGELICAL LUTHERAN—520 Clay. Rev. O. Praetorius, pastor. Services at 10 a. m. and 7:30 p. M. Sunday-school at 9 a. m.

GRACE ENGLISH LUTHERAN CHURCH—406 26th. Rev. C. F. Steck pastor. Services 10:30 a. m. and 7:30 p. m.

Figure 78. A page from the civic section of the 1892 Louisville city directory, showing the five Jewish congregations functioning in the city in the year of Kentucky's centennial.

160   BES   CARON'S 1892 DIRECTORY.   BEV

Best Joseph, polisher B. F. Avery & Sons, b 2503 Griffiths av
" Julius, tailor, b 1202 W. Green
" Lena, wid Christian, b 962 E. Market
" Mary, domestic 1131 Morton av
" Milton, c, lab, b 920 13th
" Samuel T., supt, r 2924 Portland av
" William H., agt Met. Life Ins. Co., b 929 W. Green
Besten Henry (Besten & Langen), r 302 W. Walnut
BESTEN & LANGEN (Henry Besten and E. O. Langen), cloaks, 538 4th
Beth Medresh Hogodel Congregation, Max Kabetzky, rabbi, 330 E. Jefferson
Bethel Charles R., trav agt A. Engelhard & Sons, b Phoenix Hotel
" Etta, c, nurse Willow, nw cor Longest
" James J. (Bethel & Co.), b 115 E. Jacob av
" Jeremiah, c, porter Dolph Mathey & Co., b 1129 Magazine
" John S. (J. S. Bethel & Co.), b 523 W. Chestnut
" Joseph C. (Carter Bros. & Co.), r 115 E. Jacob av
" J. S. & Co. (J. S. Bethel), leaf tobacco, 215 11th
" Laura, c, laundress, b 708 York
" Martha, c, domestic 717 8th, b 717 9th
" Robert, c, lab, r 717 9th
" William H., engineer N. N. & M. V. Co., b 1519 Southgate
" & Co.(J. J. Bethel), tobacco rehandlers, 601 10th
Betschart Joseph D., lab, b 814 Baxter av
" Mary Mrs., r 814 Baxter av
Bettag Annie, cook 1346½ 2d
" Louisa, cook 1338 3d
Bettinger John, painter L. & N., r N. A
Bettison David C.,clk,b 1603 W. Broadway
" Percy R., civil engineer L. & N., r 1521 21st
Bettler Rosa, domestic 520 W. Breckinridge
Betts George C. Rev., rector Grace Episcopal Church, r 321 E. Gray
" John, bkkpr Head & Head, b 831 7th
Betz Albert, lab Hall & Hayward Co., b 331 1st
" Carl, carpenter Siemens & Hommrich, b 1605 Hancock
" Charles (Ackerman & Betz), b 517 Clay
" Conrad G., clk Boone Paper Co., b 517 Clay
" Emma, tailoress Kahn Bros., b 1718 Hancock
" Frederick, wagonmnfr, 937 E. Main
" Frederick G., stenog Martin Byrne & Son, b 517 Clay
" Henry, fitter, b 517 Clay
" Joseph, packer Hess, Henle & Co., r 1718 Hancock
" Joseph J., clk Hess, Henle & Co., b 1718 Hancock

Betz J. Gottlieb, shoemkr 517 Clay
" Margaret, wid Adam, r 730 Lampton
" Sherman, sawyer Ky. Wagon Mnfg. Co., r ns Shipp av, e of 3d
BETZ, see BATES and BATTS
Betzen Emma Mrs., r 311 W. Jefferson
" Jacob, upholsterer J. B. Herm
Betzhold Barbara, seamstress E. Hall, b 525 E. Kentucky
" Christina, domestic 143 W. Market
" Henry, carpenter J. N. Struck & Bro., r 525 E. Kentucky
Beuerlein Joseph, tailor, r 909 E. Market
Beulke Pauline Mrs., laundress, b 1815 W. Broadway
Beumer Joseph D., watchman Southwestern Iron Wks., r 1887 7th
Beushause Augusta, wid Andrew, r 1917 W. Market
" Frank W., tobacco, r 1917 W. Market
Beutel Frederick, lab O. & M
" G. Philip, physician, 321 Jackson
" Matthias, lab J. Schwarzwalder & Sons
" Rosa, domestic C. Barfield
Beuther Adam, pres The A. Beuther Fur. Co., r 217 E. Breckinridge
" A. Furniture Co. The, Adam Beuther, pres; Lawrence E. Beuther, sec. and treas; George Beuther, supt, 1403 to 1411 Preston
" Conrad cabinetmkr, r 2418 W. Market
" George, supt The A. Beuther Fur.Co., r 436 E. Kentucky
" George L., cabinetmkr Lou. Mnfg Co., r 2617 Grayson
" Jacob, stonemason J. Diebold & Sons, b 2418 W. Market
" Lawrence E., sec and treas The A. Beuther Fur. Co., r 217 E. Breckinridge
" Lena, tailoress B. Schneider, r ns Grayson, w of 26th
" Lizzie, domestic 2415 W. Market
" Mamie, tailoress B. Schneider, r ns Grayson, w of 26th
" William F., apprentice J. H. Kuhn, b 2418 W. Market
BEUTHER, see BUETER
Beutiller Rosa, domestic 2112 W. Market
Beuttenmiller Charles, plumber, b 1232 E. Jacob av
Bevan Benjamin, solicitor Provident Sav. Life Assurance Society, b 115 W. Chestnut
Beverly Emma, c, laundress, b 931 7th
" Henry W., c, hostler, r 931 7th
" Lucy, c, domestic 1123 Floyd, b 309 Pearl av
" Major, c, peddler, r 1424 Calhoun
" Mary, c, domestic 2123 3d, b 309 Pearl
" Robert, c, servant 1052 3d
" Sallie, c, laundress, r 309 Pearl av

Figure 79. A page from the alphabetic listings in the 1892 Louisville city directory, showing an entry for Beth Hamedrash Hagodol in a variant spelling. Note that Beth Israel is not listed here, indicating the perils of relying on any one source in tracing the history of congregations and synagogues.

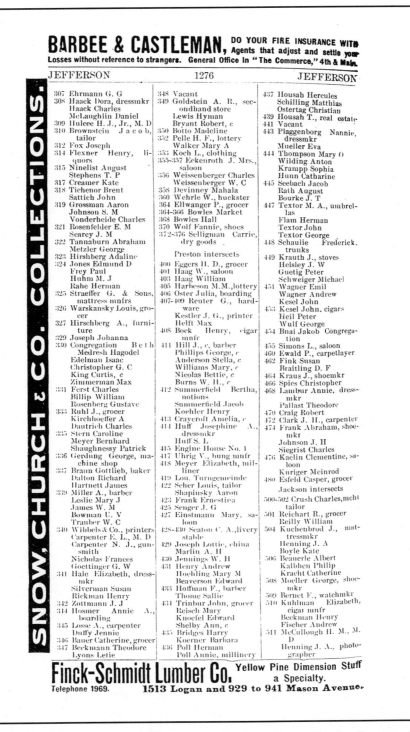

JEFFERSON	1276	JEFFERSON
307 Ehrmann G. G	348 Vacant	437 Housab Hercules
308 Haack Dora, dressmkr	349 Goldstein A. R., sec-	Schilling Matthias
Haack Charles	ondhand store	Ostertag Christian
McLaughlin Daniel	Lewis Hyman	439 Housah T., real estate
309 Hulcee H. J., Jr., M. D	Bryant Robert, c	441 Vacant
310 Brownstein Jacob,	350 Botto Madeline	443 Plaggenborg Nannie,
tailor	352 Pelle H. F., lottery	dressmkr
312 Fox Joseph	Walker Mary A	Mueller Eva
314 Flexner Henry, li-	353 Koch L., clothing	444 Thompson Mary O
quors	355-357 Eckenroth J. Mrs.,	Wilding Anton
315 Ninelist August	saloon	Krampp Sophia
Stephens T. P	356 Weissenberger Charles	Hunn Catharine
317 Creamer Kate	Weissenberger W. C	445 Seebach Jacob
318 Tichenor Brent	358 Devinney Mahala	Rath August
Sattich John	360 Wehrle W., huckster	Bourke J. T
319 Grossman Aaron	364 Ellwanger P., grocer	447 Textor M. A., umbrel-
Johnson S. M	364-366 Bowles Market	las
Vonderheide Charles	368 Bowles Hall	Flam Herman
321 Rosenfelder E. M	370 Wolf Fannie, shoes	Textor John
Searcy J. M	372-376 Selligman Carrie,	Textor George
322 Tannaburn Abraham	dry goods	448 Schaulie Frederick,
Metzler George		trunks
323 Hirshberg Adaline	Preston intersects	449 Krauth J., stoves
324 Jones Edmund D	400 Eggers H. D., grocer	Helsley J. W
Frey Paul	401 Haag W., saloon	Guetig Peter
Huhm M. J	403 Haag William	Schweiger Michael
Rahe Herman	405 Harbeson M.M.,lottery	451 Wagner Emil
325 Straeffer G. & Sons,	406 Oster Julia, boarding	Wagner Andrew
mattress mnfrs	407-409 Reuter G., hard-	Kesel John
326 Warskansky Louis, gro-	ware	453 Kesel John. cigars
cer	Kestler J. G., printer	Heil Peter
327 Hirschberg A., furni-	Helft Max	Wulf George
ture	408 Bock Henry, cigar	454 Bnai Jakob Congrega-
329 Joseph Johanna	mnfr	tion
330 Congregation Beth	411 Hill J., c, barber	455 Simons L., saloon
Medresh Hagodel	Phillips George, c	460 Ewald P., carpetlayer
Edelman Isaac	Anderson Stella, c	462 Fink Susan
Christopher G. C	Williams Mary, c	Braitling D. F
King Curtis, c	Nicolas Bettie, c	464 Kraus J., shoemkr
Zimmerman Max	Burns W. H., c	466 Spies Christopher
331 Ferst Charles	412 Summerfield Bertha,	468 Lambur Annie, dress-
Billip William	notions	mkr
Rosenberg Gustave	Summerfield Jacob	Pallast Theodore
333 Ruhl J., grocer	Koehler Henry	470 Craig Robert
Kirchhoeffer A	413 Craycroft Amelia, c	472 Clark J. H., carpenter
Dautrich Charles	414 Huff Josephine A.,	474 Frank Abraham, shoe-
335 Stern Caroline	dressmkr	mkr
Meyer Bernhard	Huff S. L	Johnson J. H
Shaughnessy Patrick	415 Engine House No. 1	Siegrist Charles
336 Gerdung George, ma-	417 Uhrig V., bung mnfr	476 Kaelin Clementine, sa-
chine shop	418 Meyer Elizabeth, mil-	loon
337 Braun Gottlieb, baker	liner	Kuriger Meinrod
Dalton Richard	419 Lou. Turngemeinde	480 Esfeld Casper, grocer
Hartnett James	422 Scher Louis, tailor	Jackson intersects
339 Miller A., barber	Shapinsky Aaron	500-502 Crush Charles,mcht
Leslie Mary J	423 Frank Ernestina	tailor
James W. M	425 Senger J. G	501 Reichart R., grocer
Bowman U. V	427 Einstmann Mary, sa-	Reilly William
Trauber W. C	loon	504 Kuchenbrod J., mat-
340 Wibbels & Co., printers	428-430 Seaton C. A.,livery	tressmkr
Carpenter E. L., M. D	stable	Henning J. A
Carpenter N. J., gun-	429 Joseph Lottie, china	Boyle Kate
smith	Marlin A. H	506 Beauerle Albert
Nicholas Frances	430 Jennings W. H	Kalbhen Philip
Goettinger G. W	431 Henry Andrew	Kracht Catherine
341 Hale Elizabeth, dress-	Hochling Mary M	508 Moeller George, shoe-
mkr	Beaverson Edward	mkr
Silverman Susan	433 Hoffman F., barber	509 Bernet F., watchmkr
Rickman Henry	Thome Sallie	510 Kuhlman Elizabeth,
342 Zottmann J. J	434 Trinbur John, grocer	cigar mnfr
344 Hosmer Annie A.,	Reisch Mary	Beckman Henry
boarding	Knoefel Edward	Fischer Andrew
345 Losse A., carpenter	Shelby Ann, c	511 McCullough H. M., M.
Duffy Jennie	435 Bridges Harry	D
346 Bauer Catherine, grocer	Koerner Barbara	Henning J. A., photo-
347 Beckmann Theodore	436 Poll Herman	grapher
Lyons Letie	Poll Annie, millinery	

Figure 80. A page from the street guide in the 1892 Louisville city directory. Beth Hamedrash Hagodol is shown in one of its temporary locations, with several other tenants, at 330 East Jefferson Street; B'nai Jacob (here Bnai Jakob) is shown at 454 East Jefferson.

street index (see the examples from the Louisville city directory for 1892: Figures 78, 79 and 80).

Unfortunately, complete sets of directories are impossible to find for most cities, since by their very nature these directories become outdated quickly and are frequently discarded. Still, some do survive in public libraries, and these I mined intensively for every city in Kentucky that had an organized Jewish congregation at one time or another. In a few cases, local telephone directories served as supplementary sources of information, especially where twentieth-century city directories were missing.

City directories for Louisville may be found at the Louisville Free Public Library and the University of Louisville Archives; for Lexington, at the Lexington Public Library; for Paducah at the Paducah Public Library; and for Owensboro, at the Owensboro Public Library. I checked directories for Henderson at the Henderson County Public Library; for Newport at the Campbell County Public Library; for Covington at the Kenton County Public Library; and for Ashland at the Boyd County Public Library. For other Kentucky cities that had Jewish communities, I obtained city directory information through correspondence with reference librarians in those towns.

A second resource critical to my research was the collection of historic Sanborn insurance maps. Published primarily for the use of insurance policy underwriters, these maps were produced intermittently and updated periodically by the Sanborn Map Company for hundreds of cities and towns throughout the United States beginning in 1876. They are so detailed that they had to be issued in groups, with each individual map covering only a limited section of the city being surveyed. Sanborn maps show the outline of every building standing at the time they were prepared, and for each structure they supply such details as height, construction material, heating method, and use (see Figures 5 and 82). For Kentucky's synagogues, I consulted the Louisville map series for 1892, 1905, and 1940; the Lexington map series for 1901 and 1934; the Newport map series for 1886 and 1910 (with corrections to 1938); and the Paducah map series for 1886, 1893, 1897, 1901 and 1942. Historic Sanborn maps are available on microfilm; the most extensive collection of original Sanborn maps in Kentucky is in the map room of the University of Kentucky Library.

Other maps that proved very useful for pinpointing synagogue locations in Louisville were the one bound into the *Louisville City Directory and Business Mirror for 1858-9,* which helped locate the site of the original Adath Israel synagogue, and those in the Louisville Abstract and Loan Association's *Atlas of the City of Louisville* (Louisville, 1876; reprinted 1974). I also consulted the maps in G.M. Hopkins's *Atlas of the City of Louisville, Kentucky, and Environs* (Philadelphia,

1884); and City Engineer James Harrington's 1872 map, "The City of Paducah, McCracken Co., Kentucky."

Although I sometimes used city directories and Sanborn maps simply to cross-check information uncovered elsewhere, I frequently had to track individual congregations and synagogue buildings through a whole series of directories or through several detailed maps in order to generate basic data. For example, I discussed the probable date of the demolition of Paducah's first synagogue (c. 1895) by comparing the 1893 Sanborn map series for Paducah, which shows the city's "old synagogue" as well as its handsome new temple on Broadway, with the 1897 Sanborn series, which shows a new private dwelling on the site of the original synagogue. To find the demolition date of the Agudath Achim synagogue in Louisville, I tracked that building through the city directories of the 1960s.

Perhaps the most complex mystery solved by careful examination of city directories and Sanborn maps had to do with the site of the B'nai Jacob synagogue on East Jefferson Street in Louisville. The available secondary sources are vague about where the B'nai Jacob congregation met throughout the 1890s, but indicate that its synagogue building on Jefferson Street was built around 1900. A news story in the *Louisville Courier-Journal* confirms that B'nai Jacob's synagogue was dedicated on March 24, 1901.[1] Yet contemporary city directories show that B'nai Jacob met at 454 East Jefferson Street from 1891 until 1908, and that the address of the congregation then changed to 430 or 432 East Jefferson. This seemingly contradictory information could be sorted out only by a detailed analysis of Louisville city directories from the turn of the century and a meticulous inspection of the Sanborn insurance maps from the same period. This close examination disclosed that B'nai Jacob did not really move at all between 1891 and 1927; the lot identified as 454 East Jefferson until 1908 had simply had its designation changed to 432 East Jefferson. Furthermore, a scrutiny of the maps revealed that in the period between 1891 and 1927 two different buildings had stood on the lot in question. The first (appearing on the 1892 Sanborn map) was a structure that had originally served as a church; it was 28 feet high to the eaves and heated with stoves. The second building (appearing on the 1905 Sanborn map) was a new house of worship 32 feet high, heated by a furnace. From this information it was possible to deduce that B'nai Jacob took over a church building when it first established itself on its East Jefferson Street site, and then, about ten years later, it demolished that building and constructed a new *shul* in its place.

Local histories produced during the late nineteenth and early twentieth centuries constitute yet another genre of sources useful for this study. These histories include the standard collections of city and county lore that were published ubiquitously around the turn of the century (they almost always contained some references to local Jewish organizations) and also a few works dealing with specific Jewish communities. In the first category are Josiah Stoddard Johnston's *Memorial History of Louisville from Its First Settlement to the Year 1896* (Chicago, 1896); *History of Fayette County, Kentucky*, edited by William Henry Perrin (Chicago, 1882); Edmund L. Starling's *History of Henderson County, Kentucky* (Henderson, Ky., 1887); and *History of Daviess County, Kentucky* (Chicago, 1883; reprinted Evansville, Ind., 1966). In the second category, histories of specific Jewish communities, are Isaac W. Bernheim's *History of the Settlement of Jews in Paducah and the Lower Ohio Valley* (Paducah, Ky., 1912); a slim volume compiled by the Jewish Historical Society of New Orleans, *History of the Jews of Louisville, Ky.* (New Orleans, 1901); and *History of Congregation Adath Israel, Louisville, Kentucky, and the Addresses Delivered at the Dedication of its New Temple* (Louisville, 1906).

A number of reference works produced chiefly for a Jewish readership are also sources of data on Kentucky Jewry. Chief among such works is the *American Jewish Year Book*, a publication that has now appeared annually for nearly 100 years. Several times during the twentieth century the *Year Book* compiled listings of Jewish institutions throughout the United States, and these provide valuable information about the congregations and synagogues of Kentucky (see Figure 81). The *Year Book* data most important for this study came from the volumes for the Jewish years 5668 (1907–08) and 5680 (1919–20).

Listings of Kentucky synagogues can be found as well in various guides that have appeared to serve the needs of Jewish tourists and travelers in the United States. Examples are Bernard Postal and Lionel Koppman's post–World War II volume, *A Jewish Tourist's Guide to the U.S.* (Philadelphia, 1954); and the recently compiled *Traveling Jewish in America*, by Ellen Chernofsky (Lodi, N.J., 1991). Jewish encyclopedias too contain material relating to Kentucky Jewry. The article "Kentucky" written by Lewis Dembitz for the *Jewish Encyclopedia* (New York and London, 1901–16), volume 7, is a very valuable piece; the "Kentucky" entry in the more recent *Encyclopedia Judaica* (Jerusalem, c. 1972), volume 10, is less helpful.

It is unfortunate that so few early manuscript records of Kentucky's Jewish congregations are now in existence. Because many congregations began as informal gatherings, they may not even have kept written accounts of their initial activities; where early records did once exist, they have tended to disappear as congregations disbanded, merged, or simply moved from one building to another. It is even possible that the great Ohio River flood of 1937 claimed some of the documents of congregations in river towns such as Louisville, Owensboro, and Henderson.

The only Louisville congregation that has an organized archive today is Adath Jeshurun. The newsletters, minutes, and correspondence that have been preserved and catalogued there yielded some interesting and important data on the design and construction not only of Adath Jeshurun's Woodbourne Avenue building but also of its earlier Brook Street synagogue. In Lexington, Temple Adath Israel has also organized an archive, but its holdings relate primarily to the congregation's more recent history.

The Temple on Brownsboro Road in Louisville has preserved a great deal of material relating to its brief history and also to the history of its two predecessor congregations (especially Adath Israel). Although the bulk of the material at The Temple remains uncatalogued and unorganized, my search of the collections there did uncover many items of enormous value. These include several minute books of Adath Israel's board of directors; the minute book of the congregation's Building and Finance Committee for the period 1866 to 1876; voluminous correspondence between Rabbi H.G. Enelow and the designer of Adath Israel's stained glass windows; and a whole box of documents amassed by Ben Strauss, chairman of the Adath Israel building committee when its Third Street temple was being erected.

Some manuscript materials related to the synagogues of Kentucky have found their way to the American Jewish Archives in Cincinnati, an extremely important research institution located on the campus of Reform Judaism's main rabbinic seminary, the Hebrew Union College. Especially valuable for my purposes were the archives' holdings related to Jewish life in Henderson, Harlan, Newport, and Lexington. Among the individual items of special significance are Henderson resident S.O. Heilbronner's 1942 typescript "History of the Congregation" (in the "Histories" file); the minutes of the Spinoza Burial Society in Lexington (microfilm #497); the early records of Harlan's B'nai Sholom, presented to the American Jewish Archives by the first secretary of that congregation, a physician named Harry Linden; and two manuscript reports on Kentucky Jewish communities prepared in response to a questionnaire distributed to student rabbis in 1935: a description by Myron Silverman of the Jews of Ashland, and one by Jacob Polish of the Jews of southeastern Kentucky.

It has long been the practice of Hebrew Union College to assign student rabbis to minister to small congregations throughout the United States during their senior year, and information about the periodic visits of these students to their congregations is maintained in the Ministration Files of the office of the dean of the college. I found the documents there very useful in tracing the history of several small Kentucky congregations; indeed, it was these files that led to my discovery of the short-lived Blue Grass Judean Society of Danville. And because my project revealed the potential research value of past Ministration Files from Hebrew Union College, they have now been transferred to the American Jewish Archives.

376   AMERICAN JEWISH YEAR BOOK   [Kentucky

CG.   **Hebrew Congregation.** Pres., Joseph Kamensky; Sec., John Berkowitz, 109
       N. Main. Members, 50. *Services:* Sabbath, Hebrew.
CHAR. **Associated Jewish Charities of Wichita.** Org. 1915. Pres., Henry Wallen-
       stein. Members, 50. *Constituent Societies:* Congregation Emanu El;
       Hebrew Congregation.
CEM.   **Cemetery,** Frisco Heights. Inc. 1885. Owned by Congregation Emanu El.

KENTUCKY

ASHLAND (Jewish pop. 86)

CG.   *Agudas Achim of Ashland and Catlettsburg.
EDUC. **Hebrew Sunday School.** Supt., Simon Harris.

COVINGTON (Jewish pop. 350)

CG.   **Temple Israel,** 7th and Greenup. Org. 1906. Cantor, ——— Lowenthal,
       Newport, Ky.; Pres., M. Berman; Sec., M. Mendelson. Members,
       31; income, $500. *Services:* Weekly, Hebrew and English. *School:*
       Classes, 2; teachers, 2; pupils, 25; sessions weekly, 1.

HENDERSON (Jewish pop. 275)

CG.   **Adath Israel,** Center and Alcoes. Org. 1887. Reader, Moses Heilbronner;
       Pres., Alexander Mayer; Sec., Henry Levy. Members, 26; income.
       $850. *Services:* Friday evening and Festivals, English and Hebrew.
       School: Classes, 2; teachers. 2; pupils, 17; sessions weekly, 1.
CEM.   **Cemetery.**

LEXINGTON (Jewish pop. 385)

CG.   **Adath Israel Congregation,** Maryland Av. Org. 1907. Rabbi, Jacob B.
       Krohngold; Pres., Gus. L. Heyman; Sec., Harry Klein. *Services:*
       Weekly, English and Hebrew. *School:* Classes, 4; teachers, 4; pupils,
       30; sessions weekly, 1. *Auxiliary:* Sisterhood. Sec., Mrs. I. J. Miller.
       Ahavath Zion, Maxwell. Org. 1915. Cantor, H. Hochberg. *Services:*
       Hebrew. *School:* Teachers, 1; pupils, 15; sessions weekly, 5.
       Ohavei Zion. Org. 1914. Sec., E. Rosenberg.
CHAR. **Federation of Jewish Charities,** 264 W. Main. Org. Feb. 1, 1917. Pres.,
       Simon Wolf; Sec., Gus Loeb. Members, 70; income, $1233.50.
       Temple Society. Org. 1917. Sec., Mrs. Max Kaplan.
CEM.   **Spinoza Society.** Inc. April 21, 1873. Sec., I. J. Miller. Maintains a
       cemetery used by the Jews of Lexington and of Eastern and Central
       Kentucky.

LOUISVILLE (Jewish pop. 9000)

CG.   **Adath Israel,** 834 3d Av. Org. 1843. Rabbi, Joseph Rauch; Pres., Ben S.
       Washer; Sec., Arnold Levy. *Services:* Hebrew and English. *Schools:*
       2; teachers, 18; pupils, 265; sessions weekly, 2. *Auxiliary Societies:*
       Adath Israel Sisterhood; Hebrew Ladies' Sewing Circle. Org. 1860.
       Pres., Mrs. Ben Strauss; Sec., A. Lapp.
       Adath Jeshurun, Floyd and Chestnut. Rabbi, J. J. Gittleman; Sec., Julius L.
       Khourt. *Auxiliary Society:* Ladies' Auxiliary.
       Agudath Achem, 1115 W. Jefferson. Org. 1905. Rabbi, A. L. Zarchy;
       Pres., I. Costin; Sec., L. Monfried. *Services:* Sabbath, Hebrew.
       Auxiliary Society: Ladies' Auxiliary.
       Anshe Sphard, 513 S. 1st. Rabbi, S. Klawansky; Pres., S. Fliegel; Sec.,
       Jake Cohen.
       Beth Hamedrosh Hagodol, Preston and Green. Rabbi, A. L. Zarchy; Pres.,
       A. Zimmerman; Sec., J. Bass.
       B'nai Jacob, 454 E. Jefferson. Org. 1882. Rabbi, A. L. Zarchy; Cantor, J.
       Goldberg; Pres., Leon Sher; Sec., L. Monfried. Members, 140. *Ser-
       vices:* Three times daily, Hebrew.

Figure 81 (and on pacing page). A section of the Kentucky listings in the *American Jewish Year Book* for the Jewish year 5680 (1919-20), showing an inventory of Jewish

CG. **Brith Sholom,** 2d and College. Org. 1879. Rabbi. Ign. Mueller. *Services:* Hebrew and English. *School:* Classes, 9; teachers, 9; pupils, 175; sessions weekly, 2. *Auxiliary Societies:* Ladies' Auxiliary; Ladies' Benevolent Society; Sewing Circle.
United Hebrew Orthodox Congregations. Sec., M. Kaplan, 323 E. Walnut.

EDUC. **Adath Israel Educational and Charitable Association,** 834 S. 3d. Pres., Jos. G. Sachs, Sr.
Beth Israel Society, 330 E. Walnut. Org. 1908. Pres., S. Weber; Sec., A. L. Zarchy.
Louisville Talmud Torah Society, 208 E. Walnut. Sec., J. Handmaker.
Neighborhood House, 428 South 1st. Org. Sept., 1896. Pres., E. S. Tachau; Sec., L. Allen; Headworker, Frances Ingram. Members, 1500; income, $8000.
Yiddish Literary Society, 529 S. 1st. Sec., Harris Finkelstein.
Young Men's Hebrew Association, 729 S. 2d. Org. 1890. Pres., Ben S. Washer; Sec., Louis Cohen. Members, 850; income, $10,000.

CHAR. **Bernheim Nurses' Home,** 228 E. Kentucky.
Jewish Welfare Federation. Organized 1909, as Federation of Jewish Charities of Louisville, 529 S. 1st. Pres., Victor Burger; Sec.-Supt., Mrs. Lula D. Krakaur. Members, 619; income, $33,000. *Constituent Societies:* United Hebrew Relief Association; Jewish Hospital Association; Hachnosath Orchim Society; Widows' and Orphans' Society; Hebrew Ladies' Sewing Circle; Young Ladies' Sewing Circle; Ladies' Society B'rith Sholom; Neighborhood House; Philanthropic Committee of the Council of Jewish Women; Jewish Orphan Asylum, Cleveland, O.; Sir Moses Montefiore Kesher Home, Cleveland, O.; Nat'l Jewish Hospital for Consumptives, Denver, Colo.; Jewish Consumptives' Relief Society, Denver, Colo.
Gemiluth Hessed Society, 212 S. 1st. Org. 1896. Pres., S. Moott; Sec., L. Monfried. Members, 125.
Hachnosath Orchim (Hebrew Sheltering Society), 406 S. 1st. Sec., A. Fish.
Jewish Children's Home, 1233 Garvin Pl. Matron, Annie Nevils.
Jewish Hospital Association, 105 W. Main. Pres., Sam Haas; Sec., Mrs. Lula D. Krakaur, 529 S. 1st; Supt., Clara Fisher.
Jewish Ladies' Benevolent Society, No. 1. Org. 1849. Pres., Mrs. I. A. Weis; Sec., Mrs. L. C. Edleson. Members, 200.
United Hebrew Relief Association, 1227 S. First. Pres., Gus Rosenberg.
Widows' and Orphans' Society, Weissinger-Gaulbert Bldg. Sec., Mrs. Jos. Kern.
Young Ladies' Sewing Circle, 1430 S. 2d. Sec., Mrs. Morris Greenbaum. Members, 10.
Musical Study Club. Pres., Mrs. Lewis W. Cohn, 40 Reeser Pl., Sec., Mrs. Jos. Rauch.
Standard Club Inc., 1000 3d Av. Pres., Mose Grabfelder; Sec., Jos. G. Sachs, Jr. Members, 125.

M. B. **United Society of Lodges.** Sec., Moses Arluck, 313 E. Jefferson.

CEM. **Cemetery,** 7th St. Rd. Owned by Congregation Beth Hamedrosh Hagodol.
Cemetery, Preston Rd. Owned by Congregations Adath Israel, Adath Jeshurun, and Brith Sholom.
Locust Lane Cemetery. Owned by Congregations B'nai Jacob and Anshe Sphard.

NEWPORT (Jewish pop. 300)

CG. **Ohave Sholom,** 6th and Brighton. N. Kooner.
Shaarai Zedek, 117 E. 5th. Pres., A. Colker. *Auxiliary Society:* Ladies' Auxiliary.

CHAR. **Hebrew Emergency Association,** 117 E. 5th. Pres., I. J. Riefkin.

EDUC. **Free Hebrew School,** 535 Patterson. Pres., M. Stuhlbarg.

M. B. **Hebrew Mutual Aid,** 4th and York. Sec., I. Hauer, 425 W. 5th.

ZION. **Newport Zionist Society,** 117 E. 5th. Org. 1907. Pres., H. L. Stuhlbarg; Sec., Yetta Roth. Members, 45.

organizations in the cities of Ashland, Covington, Henderson, Lexington, Louisville, and Newport.

Even though city directories, old maps, turn-of-the-century local histories, and contemporary manuscripts are certainly more reliable than personal recollections or even published secondary works, they are by no means foolproof. In the city directories that were perhaps my most fundamental sources of information, inconsistencies and inaccuracies often cropped up. Consider, for example, the difficulties of tracking the Beth Hamedrash Hagodol congregation through the Louisville city directories of the late nineteenth century. In the 1891 directory Beth Hamedrash Hagodol appears in the street guide but neither in the roster of churches nor in the alphabetical listings. In the 1892 directory the congregation is listed in all three sections. Then, in the 1893 edition, Beth Hamedrash Hagodol is placed at one address in the church listings and the alphabetical section but at a different address in the street guide.

One specific problem with city directories is that they are sometimes late in reporting changes; significant time lags could occur between the establishment or relocation of an assembly and the appearance of information reflecting that event. In the Louisville city directories the address of Adath Israel was still given as the corner of Broadway and Sixth as late as 1908, for example, even though the congregation had moved to Third Street two years earlier. Similarly, Adath Jeshurun was still listed in 1921 as being on Chestnut Street, even though it had moved to Brook and College in 1919. A more extreme example comes from Lexington: the city's Ohavay Zion congregation, founded in 1912, did not appear for the first time in the Lexington city directory until 1927.

Like city directories, maps can also contain erroneous or misleading information. In G.M. Hopkins's 1884 atlas of Louisville, for example, the synagogue building of Congregation Beth Israel is labeled "Congregational Church," and in the 1892 Sanborn insurance map series, the former church then serving as the B'nai Jacob synagogue is incorrectly labeled "Beth Israel Synagogue and School." In the 1934 Sanborn series for Lexington the Ohavay Zion synagogue is inexplicably called the "Church of Abraham Synagogue"; a correction made in 1946, however, labels the building "Ohava Zion," employing the spelling used by the congregation itself for many years.

Obviously, no individual source used for this study could be considered completely trustworthy. As a result, the preparation of this volume required not only piecing together many fragments of information collected from a variety of sources but also comparing and reconciling the often conflicting data.

Sometimes it was fairly easy to detect and account for errors in the available sources. For example, the Louisville city directory for 1911 gives the address for Agudath Achim as 606 West Broadway, when in fact the congregation was almost certainly using facilities at 606 West

Walnut that year and never had a home on West Broadway at all; this mistake was probably the result of a simple clerical error. The *American Jewish Year Book* for 5675 (1914–15) gives the name of Lexington's then newly founded congregation Ohavay Zion (Lovers of Zion) as Sharay Zion (Gates of Zion); here the inaccuracy may have been the result of misread handwriting. The *Year Book* for 5681 (1920–21) shows a Congregation Beth El in Lexington, the compilers having mistaken a city in Mississippi for the one in Kentucky.

Where individual fragments of evidence were found to be totally inconsistent with the larger picture that was emerging of a congregation's or a synagogue's history, I generally ignored the anomalous data. In a very few cases, however, it seemed appropriate at least to record the existence of a stray bit of incongruous information rather than to discard it completely. Thus, Table 2 notes alternative names for some congregations, even if they were encountered in only a single instance. The name "Brotherly Love Congregaton" surfaced only once in connection with Covington's Jewish congregation, for example, in a 1907 article in the *Kentucky Post*, and the name "Shaarai Zedek" was used to identify Newport's Fifth Street synagogue in only one reference, the *American Jewish Year Book* for 5680 (1919–20).

Occasionally, reaching a conclusion about some aspect of the story told in this book entailed a difficult decision to discount assertions made in sources that I would normally have considered quite reliable. For example, a manuscript report on Louisville's early Jewish history, prepared by an officer of the Adath Israel congregation around 1876, states that there were then three congregations serving the local community. All the other evidence, however, suggests that only Adath Israel and Beth Israel were functioning in the city during the 1870s, and so I have concluded that the 1876 report is incorrect. Similarly, the standard late nineteenth-century history of Fayette County asserts that the first Jewish congregation in Lexington was established in 1879, but I have rejected this contention on the basis of information from other sources. And one final example: other information available about southeastern Kentucky's Jewish history suggests that the report filed by Jacob Polish in 1935, after he had served as a student rabbi for the High Holidays in Middlesboro, contains several errors. Polish reports on the Jewish congregation of southeastern Kentucky as if it were based in Middlesboro rather than in Harlan, and he apparently took the date of the establishment of a Jewish cemetery in Middlesboro (1905) to be the founding date of a Jewish congregation in the town.[2]

Of course, not all errors in the sources were equally easy to discover and to address. Those that appeared in very early documents often took on a life of their own, being repeated without question in subsequent publications. For example, in 1881 the *American Israelite*, an influential journal published in Cincinnati, incorrectly identified the Jewish congregation of Owensboro as "Benai Israel" (Children of Israel) instead of Adath Israel (Congregation of Israel). This inaccuracy made its way into the 1976 handbook *Historical Churches of Daviess County*, which reports that Adath Israel was probably originally called "B'nai Israel," and the error was repeated once again in a brochure prepared by one of Adath Israel's congregants in 1984.[3]

Misinformation not only about the original name of Owensboro's congregation but also about its meetinghouse has been perpetuated in secondary sources. The standard *History of Daviess County, Kentucky* reported in 1883 that Adath Israel's temple had been built in 1878 and was "located on Lewis Street, between Fourth and Fifth." This information is incorrect on two counts. In reality, the Owensboro temple was erected in 1877, not 1878, and it does not stand on Lewis Street but rather on Daviess Street, one block away. Nonetheless, when William Foster Hayes published his *Sixty Years of Owensboro* in 1943, he repeated the incorrect address given in the standard county history, and that address was reported once again in a 1972 newspaper article published in the *Owensboro Messenger and Inquirer*. The incorrect date of construction given over a century ago in the *History of Daviess County* has also been repeated several times; it even appears on the plaque affixed to the front of the Adath Israel temple denoting its inclusion on the National Register of Historic Places.[4] The most reliable source of information about the construction of the Adath Israel temple is the 1877 account of its dedication in the *Owensboro Examiner*, an account written in the typically ornate style of nineteenth-century newspaper journalism and included as Appendix B in this book.

Sometimes, seemingly irreconcilable differences in the limited data available on a given topic made it difficult to identify and deal with errors in the sources. The published information about the original meeting place of Louisville's Adath Israel provides a case in point. The history of the congregation compiled in 1906 asserts that "in the beginning, religious services were held in one of the upper rooms of a boarding house located on Market Street between Second and Third Streets," and it reports that after Adath Israel was chartered, rooms were rented "on Main Street, near Brook." The 1918 account of Adath Israel's seventy-fifth anniversary, however, states that "three-quarters of a century ago the congregation began to worship in a vacant room over a store on Market street, between First and Second."[5]

There is similar contradictory information about when Congregation B'nai Jacob was established. Josiah Stoddard Johnston's 1896 *Memorial History of Louisville* relates that B'nai Jacob was founded on April 2, 1882, and the *American Jewish Year Book* for 5668 (1907–08) specifies the 1882 date as well. However, the historical sketch published in 1971 by Keneseth Israel (the successor congregation to B'nai Jacob) gives the date of B'nai Jacob's founding as April 27, 1887. And Herman

Landau's *Adath Louisville* reports yet a third date: according to Landau, B'nai Jacob was founded on April 20, 1877. To complicate matters even more, none of the published commentaries on B'nai Jacob's origins gives any indication as to its own sources of information.[6] Where such contradictions in the data could not be resolved conclusively, I had to make an educated guess about which of the various accounts was most likely to be accurate.

Perhaps the most fundamental difficulty in the face of inconclusive or contradictory evidence was the problem of determining whether or not certain buildings in which prayer services had been held merited inclusion in an inventory of synagogues. If the buildings in question served primarily as Jewish houses of worship, then they obviously deserved to be listed; if they were used for worship only incidentally, they did not. In this regard, the most difficult problem of identification arose in connection with the building that stood at 425 East Jefferson Street in Louisville, the structure that for a few years at the turn of the century served as the meeting place of Congregation Beth Hamedrash Hagodol (perhaps then known also as the Talmud Torah congregation).

Sanborn maps from 1892 and from 1905 both show the structure at 425 East Jefferson as a single-story dwelling, and the street guides in the city directories from the turn of the century list the schoolmaster Azariah Epstein as the occupant. This suggests that the house in question was used primarily as a Jewish school, and that its function as a congregational meeting place was only secondary. Moreover, in his 1904 essay on Kentucky for the *Jewish Encyclopedia*, Lewis Dembitz mentions a "Russian 'Minyan' [prayer group]" that is almost certainly Beth Hamedrash Hagodol, and he reports that that congregation was the only one in Louisville without its own house of worship. Still, it is possible that the dwelling at 425 East Jefferson had been converted into a synagogue and that it was the building's function as a school, and perhaps also as a residence for Epstein, that was secondary. Ultimately, the building was not included in this study's roster of Kentucky synagogues because of a decision I made early in the project: only buildings that served primarily as the homes of Jewish congregations would be considered synagogues, and these structures would have to be identified with a high degree of certainty.

There was a similar problem of identification in regard to a house at 430 West Sixth Street in Newport, which served as the meeting place of Congregation Ohave Sholom in the late 1910s and early 1920s. Nothing in the available documentary record can conclusively establish its status as a synagogue; nonetheless, in this case there was enough oral testimony and circumstantial evidence to justify placing the Sixth Street building on the inventory of Kentucky synagogues. One important piece of testimony comes from former Speaker of the Kentucky House of Representatives Morris Weintraub, a Newport attorney now retired in Florida. Describing Jewish life in Newport, he recalls that during the 1920s the synagogue of the United Hebrew Congregation was known as the "Big *Shul*": it was "considered the *Shul* for the more affluent," while "the other Jewish people had various little *Shuls* in the West End of Newport." Although there is no evidence to confirm Weintraub's memory of several little synagogues, his recollection tends to reinforce the idea that in the period just after the First World War there was at least one additional house of worship in Newport. Weintraub specifically recalls "a little place on Chestnut Street . . . which was a converted home," but he may in fact have been thinking of the little Sixth Street synagogue of Ohave Sholom, since Chestnut Street runs parallel to West Sixth Street only one block away (see Figure 82).[7]

My search for pictures of Kentucky's synagogues, like the search for basic information about these buildings and the congregations they housed, involved examining a great many sources. One goal I established early was to locate at least one visual representation of every synagogue that has ever stood in the commonwealth of Kentucky, and I almost attained that end. The only synagogue building not actually pictured in this book is the converted private dwelling of Ohave Sholom in Newport; the outlines of that building, however, are shown in Figure 82.

As the credits accompanying the photographs in this book attest, many were produced specifically for this project, and several others were taken from the published works I have already discussed as sources of historical data. A substantial number of the illustrations come from unpublished sources, however, and finding these pictures proved to be just as demanding a task as uncovering basic historical information. It required poring over dozens of illustrated town histories, local guidebooks, souvenir journals, and special-interest publications from the decades around the turn of the century, and spending many hours among the photographic files at the American Jewish Archives in Cincinnati, at the Photographic Archives of the University of Louisville, and at Louisville's Filson Club, the local historical society. Most of my searches through obscure publications and massive photographic collections went unrewarded, but that made the occasional discoveries of relevant material even more thrilling.

Finding pictures of Kentucky's very earliest synagogues was, of course, the greatest challenge. It seemed unlikely, for example, that an image of the first Adath Israel building in Louisville could be found, given that the structure had burned down in 1866. There also seemed to be little hope of locating pictures of Louisville's Beth Israel synagogue or of Paducah's Bene Yeshurum building, both of which had been abandoned by their congregations even before the turn of the twentieth century. In the end, however, I found depictions of all three. A chance conversation with Samuel Thomas, himself the author of several books

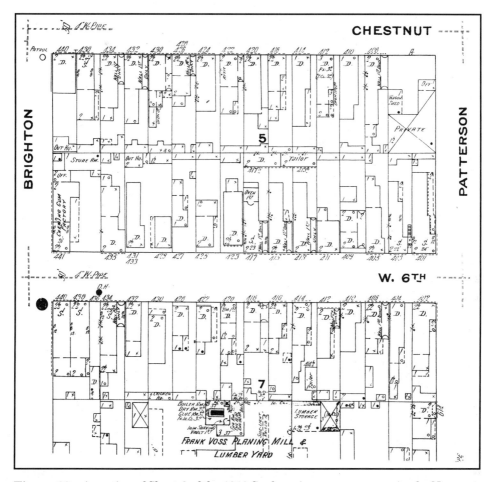

Figure 82. A portion of Sheet 8 of the 1910 Sanborn insurance map series for Newport, showing the house at 430 West Sixth Street used as a synagogue by congregation Ohave Sholom just after World War I.

about Louisville's historic neighborhoods and notable landmarks, led me to a photograph of the Beth Israel synagogue that had first appeared in an 1889 volume titled *Louisville Illustrated*. Representations of the original synagogues in Louisville and Paducah turned up in contemporary bird's-eye-view maps of those cities.

Three-dimensional bird's-eye-view maps represent a unique and important nineteenth-century art form, and they solved a potentially frustrating research problem for this study because they show not only street grids and geographic features but also views of every building in a town. Thus images of the Adath Israel synagogue of 1849 and of the Congregational Church on Jefferson Street that became the B'nai Jacob synagogue in 1891 are included in J.T. Palmatary's 1855 view of Louisville (a copy of this map hangs in the boardroom of Louisville's Liberty National Bank). Similarly, sketches of the 1871 Bene Yeshurum synagogue appear in both the 1873 map of Paducah by H. Brosius and the 1889 map of the city by J. Blanton Postlethwate (copies of these two maps are at the Market House Museum in Paducah).[8]

This discussion of methodology and sources would not be complete without some mention of the specialized literature on American synagogue history that has informed my treatment of Kentucky synagogues. Scores of individual Jewish congregations have had their histories chronicled in one form or another, most often by interested congregants or amateur historians. Unfortunately, the research done for these accounts has often been haphazard, and their perspectives have generally been quite narrow. Very few trained historians have as yet undertaken the study of local congregations (especially those in America's smaller Jewish communities), and so the scholarly study of American synagogue history is still in its infancy.

Nonetheless, several recent books have not only addressed the problems inherent in the study of synagogue history and commented on its potential value but also made some contributions to that field. Chief among these books are *The Americanization of the Synagogue, 1820–1870* by Leon A. Jick (Hanover, N.H., 1976); *American Synagogue History: A Bibliography and State-of-the-Field Survey* by Alexandra Shecket Korros and Jonathan D. Sarna (New York, 1988); and the extremely important set of essays and case studies titled *The American Synagogue: A Sanctuary Transformed*, edited by Jack Wertheimer (Cambridge, Eng., 1987). Very useful also is an article Korros and Sarna have reprinted in their volume, Daniel J. Elazar's "The Development of the American Synagogue," which appeared orginally in *Modern Judaism* 4 (October 1984). A good exploration of the current state of American synagogue history is Lance J. Sussman's "The American Synagogue: A Review Essay," *American Jewish History* 80 (Winter 1990–91).

My discussion of the various branches of American Judaism in this book is purposely very general, for it is intended only to provide background for understanding certain issues of congregational identity and synagogue design. For anyone interested in learning more about the main subdivisions of American Judaism, three very good books that provide overviews of the history and nature of American Jewry are Nathan Glazer's *American Judaism*, second edition (Chicago, 1972); Joseph L. Blau's *Judaism in America: From Curiosity to Third Faith* (Chicago, 1976); and the more recent and more controversial work by Arthur Hertzberg, *The Jews in America—Four Centuries of an Uneasy Encounter: A History* (New York, 1989). Focusing specifically on the various branches of Judaism in the United States is Marc Lee Raphael's *Profiles in American Judaism: The Reform, Conservative, Orthodox and Reconstructionist Traditions in Historical Perspective* (San Francisco, 1984). As a general introduction to American Jewish history, perhaps the best work available is the five-volume series sponsored by the

American Jewish Historical Society on the occasion of its centennial: *The Jewish People in America*, edited by Henry L. Feingold (Baltimore, 1992).

On Reform Judaism more specifically, there is Michael A. Meyer's *Response to Modernity: A History of the Reform Movement in Judaism* (New York, 1988). On Conservatism, a good reference is Marshall Sklare's *Conservative Judaism: An American Religious Movement* (New York, 1972). On Orthodox Judaism, Charles S. Liebman's "Orthodoxy in American Jewish Life" may be consulted in *American Jewish Year Book* 66 (1965). Liebman's essay is reprinted in his book *Aspects of the Religious Behavior of American Jews* (New York, 1974); that volume also contains his article "Reconstructionism in American Jewish Life." Samuel C. Heilman's *Synagogue Life: A Study in Symbolic Interaction* (Chicago, 1976) is an ethnographic and sociological study that helps elucidate the internal dynamics of contemporary Orthodox congregations in America; Riv-Ellen Prell's *Prayer & Community: The Havurah in American Judaism* (Detroit, 1989) is a useful study by an anthropologist that includes an insightful discussion of the issue of decorum in American synagogues.

Needless to say, the existing literature on American synagogue architecture was extremely important to my project. The two works that proved most significant were *Synagogue Architecture in the United States: History and Interpretations* by Rachel Wischnitzer (Philadelphia, 1955), now dated but still invaluable; and the catalogue of an exhibit at the Rose Art Museum at Brandeis University, titled *Two Hundred Years of American Synagogue Architecture* (Waltham, Mass., 1976), which contains essays by Gerald Bernstein and Gary Tinterow. Providing some insights into post–World War II issues of synagogue design was Lance J. Sussman's article "The Suburbanization of American Judaism as Reflected in Synagogue Building and Architecture, 1945–1975," *American Jewish History* 75 (September 1985). Also worthy of note are Avram Kampf's *Contemporary Synagogue Art: Developments in the United States, 1945-1965* (New York, 1966), one of the few works to raise the issue of relations between congregations and the architects they commission; and Edward Jamilly's article "The Architecture of the Contemporary Synagogue" in *Jewish Art: An Illustrated History*, edited by Cecil Roth, revised edition by Bezalel Narkiss (Greenwich, Conn., 1971).

Several picture books about synagogues in various parts of North America have appeared in the last quarter century, and they are often interesting and attractive volumes, but none of them is based on a systematic attempt to identify all the synagogues of a given environment, and none provides the kind of extensive analytic narrative that is fundamental to this study. For example, although *Treasures of a People: The Synagogues of Canada* by Sheldon Levitt, Lynn Milstone, and

Sidney T. Tenenbaum (Toronto, 1985) is based on a relatively extensive survey, it presents pictures and brief discussions only of selected Canadian synagogues. Similarly, the very well-done booklet *1843–1943— One Hundred Years of Jewish Congregations in Connecticut: An Architectural Survey*, which appeared as a special issue of the journal *Connecticut Jewish History* (Fall 1991), is limited in that it covers only buildings that were at least fifty years old in 1991 and still standing. Oscar Israelowitz's *Synagogues of New York City* (New York, 1982) and his *Synagogues of the United States* (New York, 1992) are other examples of the kinds of picture books currently available. Perhaps the best previously produced study of the synagogues of one particular locale is *The Synagogues of New York's Lower East Side*, with photograhps by Jo Renée Fine and text by Gerard R. Wolfe (New York, 1978), but its coverage too is limited, since it includes images only of synagogue buildings that could be photographed in the 1970s.

Useful for putting American synagogue architecture in a broader perspective are Carol Herselle Krinsky's *Synagogues of Europe: Architecture, History, Meaning* (Cambridge, Mass., 1985); Geoffrey Wigoder's *The Story of the Synagogue* (San Francisco, 1986); and the article "Synagogue" in the *Encyclopedia Judaica*, volume 15. The article "Art" in the *Encyclopedia Judaica*, volume 3, contains a helpful discussion of the ambivalent outlook on artistic creation of traditional Judaism; and the early twentieth-century *Jewish Encyclopedia*, volume 2, has an entire essay devoted to "Art, Attitude of Judaism toward." On American architectural styles in general, the two most useful reference works for my purposes were *American Architecture since 1780: A Guide to the Styles* by Marcus Whiffen (Cambridge, Mass., 1969); and *What Style Is It? A Guide to American Architecture*, prepared by John C. Poppeliers, S. Allen Chambers, Jr., and Nancy B. Schwartz for the National Trust for Historic Preservation (Washington, D.C., 1983).

Among the articles that address the enduring problem of finding an appropriate style for modern synagogues are Albert S. Gottlieb's "Synagogue Architecture: Can a Purely Jewish Style Be Developed in the Building of Our Temples?" *American Hebrew*, April 14, 1916, and his "Synagogue Architecture: Past and Future," *American Hebrew*, April 11, 1919; Lewis Mumford's "Towards a Modern Synagog Architecture," *Menorah Journal* 11 (June 1925); William G. Tachau's "The Architecture of the Synagogue," *American Jewish Year Book* for 5687 (1926–27); and Rachel Wischnitzer-Bernstein's "The Problem of Synagogue Architecture: Creating a Style Expressive of America," *Commentary* 3 (March 1947). Wischnitzer's article was followed by a symposium on the same theme: "Creating a Modern Synagogue Style: A Discussion," *Commentary* 3 (June 1947), with contributions by art historian Franz Landsberger and architects Ely Jacques Kahn, Eric Mendelsohn, and Percival Goodman (in collaboration with his brother Paul). Percival and Paul

Goodman also published "The Modern Artist as Synagogue Builder: Satisfying the Needs of Today's Congregations," *Commentary* 7 (Jan. 1949). The problem of appropriate design is also addressed in *An American Synagogue for Today and Tomorrow: A Guide Book to Synagogue Design and Construction*, edited by Peter Blake (New York, 1954), which was published by the Union of American Hebrew Congregations in the midst of the post–World War II synagogue building boom.

In tracing the careers of the individual architects who designed Kentucky's various synagogues, I often gleaned information from newspaper death notices. The obituary of George W. Schofield, the architect of Covington's 1915 synagogue, is in the *Cincinnati Post*, July 18, 1947; that of Leon K. Frankel, designer of Lexington's Adath Israel, is in the *Lexington Herald*, November 28, 1949; that of Leslie Moss, the architect of Covington's 1939 synagogue, is in the *Cincinnati Enquirer*, April 6, 1966; and that of Alfred S. Joseph, Jr., whose firm was involved in several Louisville synagogue projects, is in the *Louisville Courier-Journal*, February 27, 1988. For the post–World War II era the *American Architects Directory*, published in 1955, 1962, and 1970 under the sponsorship of the American Institute of Architects, was extremely helpful. Also of some use was *A History of the Profession of Architecture in Kentucky*, written by C. Julian Oberwarth with additional material by William B. Scott, Jr. (Louisville, c. 1987); and the *Biographical Dictionary of American Architects (Deceased)* by Henry F. Withey and Elsie Rathburn Withey (Los Angeles, 1956).

The resources of the Louisville Landmarks Commission proved an invaluable source of information about several architects who designed synagogues in the city of Louisville. Its files supplied data on the work of H.P. Bradshaw; McDonald and Sheblessy; James J. Gaffney; Joseph and Joseph; Wagner and Potts; and Arrasmith Judd Rapp. Also helpful was the material about architects Kenneth McDonald, John Francis Sheblessy, William J. Dodd, Arthur Cobb, and Alfred Joseph, Sr., in Marty Lyn Poynter Hedgepeth's "The Victorian and the Beaux-Arts," a master's thesis submitted in 1981 at the University of Louisville. On Brinton Davis, the architect of the 1893 Paducah temple, there is "The Hill Builder: Brinton B. Davis and Western Kentucky University," an unpublished article by Jonathan Jeffrey, a librarian at Western Kentucky University.

Finally, a few words about population statistics are in order. The earliest complete Jewish population statistics for Kentucky (and other states) appear in *Statistics of the Jews of the United States*, a booklet published by the Union of American Hebrew Congregations in Philadelphia in 1880. This compilation of data is discussed at some length in my article "The Jewish Communities of the United States on the Eve of Mass Migration: Some Comments on Geography and Bibliography," *American Jewish History* 78 (September, 1988). Twentieth-century Jewish population statistics for Kentucky (and, again, for the rest of the United States) have appeared periodically in the *American Jewish Year Book*. The volumes for the Jewish years 5675 (1914–15), 5689 (1928–29), and 5701 (1940–41) are especially useful, as is volume 52 (1951). Recently, population figures from these and several other sources have all been compiled and published together in Jacob Rader Marcus's *To Count a People: American Jewish Population Data, 1585–1984* (Lanham, Md., 1990).

Information on the very earliest Jewish settlers in Kentucky is available in an essay by Lewis N. Dembitz, "Jewish Beginnings in Kentucky," *Publications of the American Jewish Historical Society* 1 (1890); and in an article by Ira Rosenwaike, "The First Jewish Settlers in Louisville," *Filson Club History Quarterly* 53 (January 1979). Jewish migration patterns in Paducah, Owensboro, and Lexington are discussed in my article "Stability and Mobility in the Small Jewish Community: Examples from Kentucky History," *American Jewish History* 79 (Spring 1990). Demographic information on Louisville in the last decade of the twentieth century is available in Gary A. Tobin and Gabriel Berger's *The Jewish Community Federation of Louisville Demographic and Attitudinal Study* (Waltham, Mass., 1991).

Much of the early history of Kentucky Jewry has already been lost to living memory, and many of the sources of information that might have told us about Kentucky's Jewish heritage have disappeared as well. Although some early congregational minute books and publications have been preserved over many decades, much more documentary material has been lost, and many of the synagogue buildings that were once a part of the commonwealth's built environment are no longer standing. I hope that this volume, by reconstructing the historical outline of Kentucky Jewry's religious institutions and by compiling a multifaceted inventory of Kentucky's synagogue buildings, will help to preserve at least a portion of the long and fascinating history of Jewish life in the commonwealth. In doing so, this book should also help to foster an appreciation of the way in which the presence of even a relatively small Jewish population can enrich and diversify a region's religious and cultural heritage.

Tables

Table 1

The Jewish Population of Kentucky and Selected Kentucky Cities in Selected Years

	Jewish population							
	1878	1907	1927	1937	1947/48	1960	1968	1984
Kentucky	3,602	10,090	19,533	17,894		11,000	11,200	12,910
Ashland			170	150	200	175	150	
Covington			500	350				
Danville	20			25				
Harlan area				89[a]	160			
Henderson	79	150	93	88	140	140		
Hopkinsville	81		86	70	140	120	120	
Lexington	140	350	750	660	856	1,200	1,200	1,500
Louisville	2,500	8,000	12,500	13,800	9,000	8,500	8,500	9,200
Newport			600	475				
Owensboro	213	150	49	65				
Paducah	203	260	800[b]	600[b]	150	275	175	175

Sources: For 1907, estimates by Henrietta Szold as reported in *American Jewish Year Book* for 5675 (1914–15), p. 365; for all other years, Jacob Rader Marcus, *To Count a People: American Jewish Population Data, 1585–1984* (Lanham, Md., 1990), pp. 76–78.

[a] Combined figures for Harlan, Middlesboro, and Pineville.

[b] Figure is almost certainly too high. See Lee Shai Weissbach, "Stability and Mobility in the Small Jewish Community: Examples from Kentucky History," *American Jewish History* 74 (1990): 375.

Table 2

The Jewish Congregations of Kentucky, by Date of Establishment

Congregation	Dates	City	Meaning of Hebrew name	Branch[*]
Adath Israel[1]	1842–1977	Louisville	Congregation of Israel	O/R
Beth Israel[2]	1851–1894	Louisville	House of Israel	O
Adath Israel	1858–present	Owensboro	Congregation of Israel	O?/R
Temple Israel[3] (Bene Yeshurum)	1871–present	Paducah	(Children of Jeshurun)[4]	O/R
Spinoza Society[5]	1877–1904?	Lexington		R?
Brith Sholom[6]	1880–1977	Louisville	Covenant of Peace	C/R
B'nai Jacob[7]	1882–1926	Louisville	Children of Jacob	O
Beth Hamedrash Hagodol[8]	1887–1926	Louisville	Great House of Study	O
Adas Israel	1887–1966	Henderson	Congregation of Israel	R
Anshei Sfard	1893–present	Louisville	Men of Spain[9]	O
Adath Jeshurun[10]	1894–present	Louisivlle	Congregation of Jeshurun[4]	C
Agudath Achim	1896–1986	Ashland	Society of Brothers	O/R
United Hebrew Congregation[11] (Agudat Yisrael)	1897–c. 1966	Newport	(Society of Israel)	O
Adath Israel	1904–present	Lexington	Congregation of Israel	R

[*] C = Conservative; O = Orthodox; R = Reform; T = Traditional.

[1] Merged with Brith Sholom to form The Temple, 1976.

[2] Offshoot of Adath Israel; also known as the Polish House of Israel.

[3] Outgrowth of the Chevra Yeshurum Burial Society, organized 1859; the name Temple Israel replaced the name Bene Yeshurum in 1893.

[4] Jeshurun is a poetic name of Israel, emphasizing Israel's uprightness.

[5] Outgrowth of the Spinoza Burial Society, organized 1872; named in honor of the seventeenth-century Dutch Jewish rationalist philosopher Baruch (Benedict) Spinoza.

[6] Offshoot of Beth Israel; merged with Adath Israel to form The Temple, 1976.

[7] Offshoot of Beth Israel; merged with Beth Hamedrash Hagodol to form Keneseth Israel, 1926.

[8] May have been known as the Talmud Torah (Teaching of Torah) congregation, 1897–1900; merged with B'nai Jacob to form Keneseth Israel, 1926.

[9] Name derived from the use of some liturgical conventions of Spanish Jews adopted in Eastern Europe.

[10] Organized by former members of Beth Israel.

[11] May also have been associated with the name Shaarai Zedek (Gates of Righteousness).

Congregation	Dates	City	Meaning of Hebrew name	Branch[*]
Agudath Achim[12]	1905–1971	Louisville	Society of Brothers	O
Temple of Israel[13] (Hechal Yisrael)	1906–c. 1960	Covington	(Temple of Israel)	O
Brith Jacob[14]	c. 1910–c. 1919	Lexington	Covenant of Jacob	O
Adath Israel	c. 1910–1977	Hopkinsville	Congregation of Israel	C?/R
Ohavay Zion	1912–present	Lexington	Lovers of Zion	O/C
Ohave Sholom[15]	c. 1918–c. 1925	Newport	Lovers of Peace	O
House of Israel[16]	c. 1921–c. 1975	Ashland		O
Keneseth Israel[17]	1926–present	Louisville	Assembly of Israel	O/T/C
B'nai Sholom[18]	1931–1972	Harlan	Children of Peace	C
Blue Grass Judean Society	c. 1948–1950	Danville		R
Temple Israel[19]	c. 1965–c. 1972	Covington		R
The Temple[20]	1976–present	Louisville		R
Temple Shalom	1976–present	Louisville	Temple of Peace	R
Lexington Havurah	1978–present	Lexington	Lexington Fellowship	C
Beth Israel[21]	1985–present	Louisville	House of Israel	O
Adat B'nai Yisrael	1992–present	Louisville	Congregation of the Children of Israel	R

[*] C = Conservative; O = Orthodox; R = Reform; T = Traditional.

[12] Merged with Anshei Sfard, 1971.

[13] Often referred to as Temple Israel; may originally have been known as the Brotherly Love Congregation (Ahavat Achim).

[14] First listed in Lexington city directory, 1911, as Baith Jacob (House of Jacob).

[15] Offshoot of United Hebrew Congregation.

[16] Offshoot of Agudath Achim.

[17] Formed by merger of B'nai Jacob and Beth Hamedrash Hagodol.

[18] Also associated with Middlesboro, where there has been a Jewish cemetery since 1905.

[19] Separate from the Temple of Israel of 1906 but seeking to perpetuate its name.

[20] Formed by merger of Adath Israel and Brith Sholom, 1976; full name of congregation is The Temple: Congregation Adath Israel Brith Sholom.

[21] Not associated with the Beth Israel of 1851.

Table 3

The Jewish Congregations of Kentucky, by City

City	Congregation	Dates
Ashland	Agudath Achim	1896–1986
	House of Israel	c. 1921–c. 1975
Covington	Temple of Israel	1906–c. 1960
	Temple Israel	c. 1965–c. 1972
Danville	Blue Grass Judean Society	c. 1948–1950
Harlan	B'nai Sholom	1931–1972
Henderson	Adas Israel	1887–1966
Hopkinsville	Adath Israel	c. 1910–1977
Lexington	Spinoza Society	1877–1904?
	Adath Israel	1904–present
	Brith Jacob	c. 1910–c. 1919
	Ohavay Zion	1912–present
	Lexington Havurah	1978–present
Louisville	Adath Israel	1842–1977
	Beth Israel	1851–1894
	Brith Sholom	1880–1977
	B'nai Jacob	1882–1926
	Beth Hamedrash Hagodol	1887–1926
	Anshei Sfard	1893–present
	Adath Jeshurun	1894–present
	Agudath Achim	1905–1971
	Keneseth Israel	1926–present
	The Temple	1976–present
	Temple Shalom	1976–present
	Beth Israel	1985–present
	Adat B'nai Yisrael	1992–present
Newport	United Hebrew Congregation	1897–c. 1966
	Ohave Sholom	c. 1918–c. 1925
Owensboro	Adath Israel	1858–present
Paducah	Temple Israel (Bene Yeshurum)	1871–present

Table 4

Kentucky Synagogue Sites, by Date of Occupancy

Occupied	Congregation(s)	City	Location
1849–1866	Adath Israel	Louisville	E. side Fourth St. between Green[1] and Walnut[2]
1857–1894	Beth Israel	Louisville	127 W. Green St. between First and Second
1868–1906	Adath Israel	Louisville	S.E. corner Broadway and Sixth St.
1871–1893	Bene Yeshurum	Paducah	E. side Chestnut[3] between Clark and Adams
1877–present	Adath Israel	Owensboro	429 Daviess St. at Fifth
1881–1959	Brith Sholom, then Anshei Sfard	Louisville	509 S. First St. between Walnut[2] and Chestnut[4]
1891–1927	B'nai Jacob	Louisville	432 E. Jefferson St. between Preston and Jackson[5]
1892–1966	Adas Israel	Henderson	635 Center St. at Alves
1893–1963	Temple Israel	Paducah	702 Broadway
1894–1919	Adath Jeshurun	Louisville	240 E. Chestnut St. at Floyd
1903–1950	Brith Sholom	Louisville	753 S. Second St. at College
1905–1966	United Hebrew Congregation	Newport	117 Fifth St. between Saratoga and Monmouth
1905–1926	Adath Israel	Lexington	529 Maryland Ave.
1905–1929	Beth Hamedrash Hagodol, then Keneseth Israel	Louisville	339 S. Preston St. at Green[6]
1906–1977	Adath Israel	Louisville	832 S. Third St.
1914–1986	Ohavay Zion	Lexington	120 W. Maxwell St. at Jersey

(Continued)

[1] Now Liberty.
[2] Now Muhammed Ali.
[3] Now South Fifth.
[4] Before street renumbering in the early twentieth century, address of this site was 613 First St.
[5] Between 1891 and 1900, the congregation used a former church building on this site; that building was demolished and replaced by a new synagogue, dedicatd in 1901.
[6] From c. 1905 to c. 1908 the congregation was housed in a building on this property; that building's address was then 419 Green St. (now Liberty).

Table 4, (*Continued*)

Occupied	Congregation	City	Location
1915–1937	Temple of Israel	Covington	107 E. Seventh St. between Greenup and Scott
1917–1964	Agudath Achim	Louisville	1115 W. Jefferson St.
c. 1918–c. 1925	Ohave Sholom	Newport	430 W. Sixth St.
1919–1957	Adath Jeshurun	Louisville	757 S. Brook St. at College
1925–1977	Adath Israel	Hopkinsville	Sixth St. between Clay and Liberty
1926–present	Adath Israel	Lexington	124 N. Ashland Ave.
1929–1964	Keneseth Israel	Louisville	232 E. Jacob Ave. at Floyd
1938–1986	Agudath Achim	Ashland	2411 Montgomery Ave.
1939–1973	Temple of Israel	Covington	1040 Scott St.
1947–1976	House of Israel	Ashland	2101 Carter Ave.
1950-1980	Brith Sholom, then The Temple	Louisville	1649 Cowling Ave. at Maryland[7]
1957–present	Adath Jeshurun	Louisville	2401 Woodbourne Ave. at Ellerbe
1958–present	Anshei Sfard	Louisville	3700 Dutchmans Lane
1963–present	Temple Israel	Paducah	332 Joe Clifton Dr.
1964–present	Keneseth Israel	Louisville	2531 Taylorsville Rd.
1980–present	The Temple	Louisville	5101 Brownsboro Rd. at Lime Kiln
1981–1989	Temple Shalom	Louisville	4220 Taylorsville Rd.
1985–present	Beth Israel (1985)	Louisville	1663 Almara Circle[8]
1986–present	Ohavay Zion	Lexington	2048 Edgewater Ct.
1989–present	Temple Shalom	Louisville	4615 Lowe Rd.

[7] From 1950 to 1951, while new construction was underway, congregation used a mansion on this property that had formerly housed a girls' school.

[8] The building at this site is commonly known as "The White House."

Table 5

The Life Course of Kentucky's Synagogue Buildings

Synagogue Building	Occupied as synagogue	Immediate former use	Immediate subsequent use	Demolished
Adath Israel Fourth St., Louisville	1849–1866	none (built as synagogue)	none (destroyed by fire)	1866
Beth Israel W. Green St., Louisville	1857–1894	none (built as synagogue)	Baptist church	1911
Adath Israel Broadway, Louisville	1868–1906	none (built as synagogue)	Methodist church	1942
Bene Yeshurum Chestnut St., Paducah	1871–1893	none (built as synagogue)	none (razed for private home)	c. 1895
Adath Israel Daviess St., Owensboro	1877–present	none (built as synagogue)	none (currently a synagogue)	still standing
Brith Sholom/Anshei Sfard S. First St., Louisville	1881–1959	none (built as synagogue)	none (razed for expressway)	1962
B'nai Jacob E. Jefferson St., Louisville	1891–1900	Congregational church	none (razed for new synagogue)	1900
Adas Israel Center St., Henderson	1892–1966	none (built as synagogue)	Pentecostal church	still standing
Temple Israel Broadway, Paducah	1893–1963	none (built as synagogue)	none (razed for parking lot)	1963
Adath Jeshurun E. Chestnut St., Louisville	1894–1919	Christian church	Bible institute	c. 1937
B'nai Jacob E. Jefferson St., Louisville	1901–1927	none (built as synagogue)	private club	c. 1962
Brith Sholom Second St., Louisville	1903–1949	Baptist church	church	c. 1965
United Hebrew Congregation Fifth St., Newport	1905–1966	Christian church	Apostolic church	still standing

(Continued)

Table 5, (*Continued*)

Synagogue Building	Occupied as synagogue	Immediate former use	Immediate subsequent use	Demolished
Beth Hamedrash Hagodol/ Keneseth Israel S. Preston St., Louisville	1905–1929	German Lutheran church	Volunteers of America shelter	1964
Adath Israel Maryland Ave., Lexington	1905–1924	German Lutheran church	Christian church	still standing
Adath Israel S. Third St., Louisville	1906–1977	none (built as synagogue)	Apostolic church	still standing
Ohavay Zion Maxwell St., Lexington	1914–1986	Presbyterian church	restaurant	still standing
Temple of Israel E. Seventh St., Covington	1915–1937	none (built as synagogue)	none (razed for post office)	1938
Agudath Achim W. Jefferson St., Louisville	1917–1964	Episcopal church	none (razed for fire station)	c. 1964
Ohave Sholom West Sixth St., Newport	c. 1918–c. 1925	private home?	private home?	pre-1938
Adath Jeshurun Brook and College, Louisville	1919–1957	none (built as synagogue)	Unity church	still standing
Adath Israel Sixth St., Hopkinsville	1925–1977	none (built as synagogue)	none (roof collapsed)	1977
Adath Israel Ashland Ave., Lexington	1926–present	none (built as synagogue)	none (currently a synagogue)	still standing
Keneseth Israel E. Jacob Ave., Louisville	1929–1964	none (built as synagogue)	interdenomi- national church	still standing
Agudath Achim Montgomery Ave., Ashland	1938–1986	none (built as synagogue)	Pentecostal church	still standing

Synagogue Building	Occupied as synagogue	Immediate former use	Immediate subsequent use	Demolished
Temple of Israel Scott St., Covington	1939–1973	none (built as synagogue)	Church of God	still standing
House of Israel Carter Ave., Ashland	1947–1976	none (built as synagogue)	insurance office	still standing
Brith Sholom/The Temple Cowling Ave., Louisville	1951–1980	none (built as synagogue)	Pentecostal church	still standing
Adath Jeshurun Woodbourne Ave., Louisville	1957–present	none (built as synagogue)	none (currently a synagogue)	still standing
Anshei Sfard Dutchmans Lane, Louisville	1958–present	none (built as synagogue)	none (currently a synagogue)	still standing
Temple Israel Joe Clifton Drive, Paducah	1963–present	none (built as synagogue)	none (currently a synagogue)	still standing
Keneseth Israel Taylorsville Rd., Louisville	1964–present	none (built as synagogue)	none (currently a synagogue)	still standing
The Temple Brownsboro Rd., Louisville	1980–present	none (built as synagogue)	none (currently a synagogue)	still standing
Temple Shalom Taylorsville Rd., Louisville	1981–1989	private home	private home	still standing
Beth Israel Almara Circle, Louisville	1985–present	private home	none (currently a synagogue)	still standing
Ohavay Zion Edgewater Ct., Lexington	1986–present	none (built as synagogue)	none (currently a synagogue)	still standing
Temple Shalom Lowe Road, Louisville	1989–present	none (built as synagogue)	none (currently a synagogue)	still standing

Table 6

Kentucky Congregations in Alphabetical Order and Their Synagogue Sites

Congregation	City	Founded	Synagogues
Adas Israel	Henderson	1887	635 Center St. (1892–1966)
Adat B'nai Yisrael	Louisville	1992	none
Adath Israel	Hopkinsville	c. 1910	Sixth St. (1925–1977)
Adath Israel	Lexington	1904	529 Maryland Ave. (1905–1924) 124 N. Ashland Ave. (1926–)
Adath Israel	Louisville	1842	Fourth St. (1849–1866) Broadway and Sixth (1868–1906) 832 S. Third St. (1906–1977)
Adath Israel	Owensboro	1858	429 Daviess St. (1877–)
Adath Jeshurun	Louisville	1894	228 E. Chestnut St. (1894–1919) 757 S. Brook St. (1919–1957) 2401 Woodbourne Ave. (1957–)
Agudath Achim	Ashland	1896	2411 Montgomery Ave. (1938–1986)
Agudath Achim	Louisville	1905	1115 W. Jefferson St. (1917–1964)
Anshei Sfard	Louisville	1893	613 First St. (1903–1958) 3700 Dutchmans Lane (1958–)
Beth Hamedrash Hagodol	Louisville	1887	339 S. Preston St. (1905–1926)
Beth Israel	Louisville	1851	127 W. Green St. (1857–1894)
Beth Israel	Louisville	1985	1663 Almara Circle (1985–)
Blue Grass Judean Society	Danville	c. 1948	none
B'nai Jacob	Louisville	1882	454 E. Jefferson St. (1891–1927)

Congregation	City	Founded	Synagogues
B'nai Sholom	Harlan	1931	none
Brith Jacob	Lexington	c. 1910	none
Brith Sholom	Louisville	1880	613 First St. (1881–1903) 753 S. Second St. (1903–1950) 1649 Cowling Ave. (1950–1977)
House of Israel	Ashland	c. 1921	2101 Carter Ave. (1947–c. 1976)
Keneseth Israel	Louisville	1926	339 S. Preston St. (1926–1929) 232 E. Jacob Ave. (1929–1964) 2531 Taylorsville Rd. (1964–)
Lexington Havurah	Lexington	1978	none
Ohavay Zion	Lexington	1912	120 W. Maxwell St. (1914–1986) 2048 Edgewater Ct. (1986–)
Ohave Sholom	Newport	c. 1918	430 W. Sixth St. (c. 1918–c. 1925)
Spinoza Society	Lexington	1877	none
Temple Israel	Covington	c. 1965	none
Temple Israel (Bene Yeshurum)	Paducah	1871	Chestnut St. (1871–1893) 702 Broadway (1893–1963) 332 Joe Clifton Dr. (1963–)
Temple of Israel	Covington	1906	107 E. Seventh St. (1915–1937) 1040 Scott St. (1939–1973)
Temple Shalom	Louisville	1976	4220 Taylorsville Rd. (1981–1989) 4615 Lowe Rd. (1989–)
The Temple	Louisville	1976	1649 Cowling Ave. (1977–1980) 5101 Brownsboro Rd. (1980–)
United Hebrew Congregation	Newport	1897	117 E. Fifth St. (1905–1966)

Table 7

Buildings Constructed as Synagogues in Kentucky and Their Architects

Synagogue building	First occupied	Principal design architect/firm
Adath Israel Fourth St., Louisville	1849	unknown
Beth Israel W. Green St., Louisville	1857	unknown
Adath Israel Broadway and Sixth, Louisville	1868	H.P. Bradshaw (Louisville); annex, Dodd and Cobb (Louisville)
Bene Yeshurum Chestnut St., Paducah	1871	unknown
Adath Israel Daviess St., Owensboro	1878	unknown
Brith Sholom/Anshei Sfard S. First St., Louisville	1881	unknown
Adas Israel Center St., Henderson	1892	unknown
Temple Israel Broadway, Paducah	1893	Brinton B. Davis (Paducah)
B'nai Jacob E. Jefferson St., Louisville	1901	unknown
Adath Israel S. Third St., Louisville	1906	McDonald and Sheblessy (Louisville)
Temple of Israel E. Seventh St., Covington	1915	George W. Schofield (Covington)
Adath Jeshurun Brook and College, Louisville	1919	James J. Gaffney of Gaffney and Epping (Louisville)
Adath Israel Sixth St., Hopkinsville	1925	Wolf Geller (Hopkinsville) [not a professional architect]
Adath Israel Ashland Ave., Lexington	1926	L.K. Frankel of Frankel and Curtis (Lexington); addition, Johnson Romanowitz (Lexington)

Synagogue building	First occupied	Principal design architect/firm
Keneseth Israel E. Jacob Ave., Louisville	1929	Joseph and Joseph (Louisville)
Agudath Achim Montgomery Ave., Ashland	1938	unknown
Temple of Israel Scott St., Covington	1939	Leslie E. Moss (Cincinnati)
House of Israel Carter Ave., Ashland	1947	unknown
Brith Sholom/The Temple Cowling Ave., Louisville	1951	Walter Wagner and Joseph Potts (Louisville)
Adath Jeshurun Woodbourne Ave., Louisville	1957	Sigmund Braverman of Braverman and Halperin (Cleveland); addition, Joseph and Joseph (Louisville)
Anshei Sfard Dutchmans Lane, Louisville	1958	Joseph and Joseph (Louisville)
Temple Israel Joe Clifton Drive, Paducah	1963	Pepinsky, Grau, Shroud, and Shorr (Cincinnati)
Keneseth Israel Taylorsville Rd., Louisville	1964	Robert A. Nolan of Thomas J. Nolan and Sons (Louisville); additions, Joseph and Joseph (Louisville) and Gerald Baron (Louisville)
The Temple Brownsboro Rd., Louisville	1980	John Chovan of Arrasmith Judd Rapp (Louisville) in joint venture with Joseph and Joseph (Louisville)
Ohavay Zion Edgewater Ct., Lexington	1986	Pearson, Bender and Jolly (Lexington)
Temple Shalom Lowe Road, Louisville	1989	Gerald Baron (Louisville)

Appendices

Appendix A

A Newspaper Account of the Destruction of Kentucky's First Synagogue

FIRE.
Terrible Conflagration.
Louisville Theater Burned Down.
Jewish Synagogue and School Nearly Destroyed.
Loss over Eighty Thousand Dollars.
Scenes on the Ground.
Third Street Well in Flames.

About 12 o'clock last night, only some fifteen minutes after the play ended, fire broke out in the scene room of the Louisville Theater. Four or five men were in the . . . building at the time, and though but a small blaze when first seen, these persons had barely gone out of the theater to give the alarm when the inflammable material of scenery and properties were on fire, and the flames were bursting through the rear windows. Some difficulty was met with in finding the key of the nearest alarm box, and before the alarm could be sounded the building was on fire in every part, and before the engines could get water on it was manifestly past extinction. Long columns of red flame shot from all the windows and from the roof . . . .

The drinking saloon and Winter Garden were soon consumed, and the Jewish Synagogue was on fire all over the roof, and small fires were beginning to appear over the roof of the schoolhouse in the rear of the Synagogue.

The engine from Portland reached the scene in twenty-eight minutes from the sounding of the second alarm, and in two minutes more was in action.

166 \ The Synagogues of Kentucky

The synagogue would have been saved but for a strange accident. Soon after the engine No. 1 had taken position at the cistern on Third Street, between Green [now Liberty] and Walnut [now Muhammad Ali], a most excellent position from which to operate, flames burst from the mouth of the cistern, driving away the firemen and bystanders. It was like looking into the crater of a volcano. To fill the cistern with water from the nearest hydrant and override the gas required an hour's work.

Source: *Louisville Daily Courier*, October 13, 1866, p. 1.

Appendix B

A Newspaper Account of the Dedication of the Synagogue in Owensboro

"By Their Works Ye Shall Know Them."

Completion and Dedication of the Jewish Synagogue

An Enduring Monument to the Enterprise
and Liberality of Our Israelitish Citizens

Owensboro numbers among its thrifty populace a goodly sprinkle of Israelitish people. From one end of Main street to the other their business banners will be found upon the outer walls. Indeed, the largest dry goods store in the place is owned and operated by Israelitish people—the Messrs. Rothchild. A number of other first-class dry goods and clothing houses, conducted by Jewish people, may also be found upon Main and other business thoroughfares; and it is a just compliment to say that the city owes much of its commercial reputation to the vim and enterprise of this class of people. A few of them own the buildings in which they transact their business, others own the property in which they live, and others at this time are putting up fine residences on Fourth street.

Some two years ago the Israelitish people made a move looking toward the erection of a synagogue in Owensboro. Accordingly, grounds were purchased, architectural plans obtained, and to-day a handsome Jewish temple occupies the site at the corner of Fifth and Daviess streets.

A fortnight or more ago active preparations began for dedicating the house. The best musical talent in the city was brought into requisition, and the programme usual upon such occasions mapped out. Friday, August 10, was the day appointed for the dedicatory ceremonies, and the hour, 4:30 p.m., found a multitude of people awaiting the inauguration of the ceremonies.

Precisely at 40 minutes past 4 the male membership, preceded by a bevy of little girls, filed down one of the aisles to the pulpit. Three of the latter—Misses Jennie Wile, Teresa Godshaw and Rosa Baer [—] entered the pulpit and went through the formality of turning over the temple's key, each delivering in magnificent style short and appropriate addresses.

Rev. Dr. Witamer, of Evansville, [Indiana,] to whom belonged the honor of leading in the dedicatory exercises, then read the eighth chapter of Kings, following with an earnest prayer in behalf of the membership and all others who aided by money in the construction of the house. The dedicatory sermon, which was delivered in English, and in most impressive style, was founded upon the language as contained in First Kings, 6th chapter and 12th verse. The sermon occupied about forty minutes in its delivery and was attentively listened to throughout.

The entire exercises were of a most imposing nature, and especially interesting to those unacquainted with the Jewish mode of worship.

Very general credit will be accorded the plucky congregation, who, right in the thickest of the political and financial troubles of the country, have succeeded in building in our midst a house of divine worship hardly second to any in the city.

Source: *Owensboro Examiner*, August 17, 1877.

Notes

Introduction

1. The best source of information on the founding of Louisville's Adath Israel is Charles Goldsmith, "History of Congregation Adath Israel, Part I," in *History of Congregation Adath Israel, Louisville, Kentucky, and the Addresses Delivered at the Dedication of Its New Temple* (Louisville, 1906), pp. 13–14.

2. The best source of information on the founding of Lexington's Adath Israel is the Adath Israel Minute Book for 1903–09, at the American Jewish Archives, Cincinnati (box 673).

3. The establishment of southeastern Kentucky's B'nai Sholom is described in correspondence from Harry Linden in the file "Harlan, Ky.—Congregation B'nai Sholom," at the American Jewish Archives, Cincinnati (Small Collection).

4. "Preface" to Jack Wertheimer, ed., *The American Synagogue: A Sanctuary Transformed* (Cambridge, Eng., 1987), p. vii.

5. See *American Jewish Year Book* for 5680 (1919–20), p. 377.

6. Ibid.

Chapter 1. The Formation of Kentucky's Jewish Congregations

1. Charles Goldsmith, "History of Congregation Adath Israel," p. 17.

2. On Shaar Hashomaim and the Highlands Orthodox prayer group, see Herman Landau, *Adath Louisville: The Story of a Jewish Community* (Louisville, 1981), pp. 8, 80. On the northern Kentucky group, see, for example, "List, Duo's Dedication Pull 60 Together for Rituals of their Faith," *Cincinnati Post*, March 19, 1983; and "Jews Enjoy Festival," *Cincinnati Post*, Sept. 30, 1985.

3. See Rabbi Chester Diamond of The Temple, letter to Dianne Wells of the Kentucky Historical Society, Sept. 22, 1992 (copy in possession of the author). On the adoption of Reform at Adath Israel, the best source is Goldsmith, "History of Congregation Adath Israel," pp. 16–19.

4. On the adoption of Reform in Paducah, the best source is Isaac W. Bernheim, *History of the Settlement of Jews in Paducah and the Lower Ohio Valley* (Paducah, Ky., 1912), pp. 67–69.

5. The history of the Ashland congregations is best summarized in Harold Freedman of Ashland, letter to the author, June 13, 1990.

6. The standard account of the creation of the Chevra Yeshurum Burial Society and of Bene Yeshurum is in Bernheim, *History of the Settlement of Jews*, pp. 29, 56–70.

7. Entry of Oct. 28, 1877, Spinoza Burial Society Minute Book at the American Jewish Archives, Cincinnati (Microfilm #497). See also Moses Kaufman,

History of the Spinoza Society (Lexington, Ky., 1887), a pamphlet which, strangely, does not mention the society's functions as a congregation.

8. The following discussions of Beth Hamedrash Hagodol, Anshei Sfard, and Agudath Achim in their early years are based primarily on information culled from Louisville city directories. For a discussion of these reference volumes and for more on tracing the history of individual congregations, see this book's bibliographical essay, "Discovering Kentucky's Synagogues."

9. Frieda J. Dannheiser, ed., *The History of Henderson County, Kentucky* (Evansville, Ind., 1980), p. 301; Leslie A. Lassetter, "Covington's Schule, The Temple of Israel" (research paper on file at the Kenton County Public Library, 1976), pp. 7, 13; Ashland city directories; and Saul Kaplan of Ashland, telephone interview with author, Feb. 21, 1990.

10. See "New Jewish Temple for Covington," *Kentucky Post,* Jan. 8, 1915.

11. For the first two Adath Israel buildings, see Goldsmith, "History of Congregation Adath Israel," pp. 15, 21; information on the third building is from the 1906 typescript report of the Adath Israel subcommittee on seating, on deposit at The Temple, Louisville.

12. For Hopkinsville, see "Rebuilding of Jewish Synagogue Is Unlikely," *Kentucky New Era*, Nov. 7, 1977; for Lexington, Gloria Travis Katz, ed., *Seventy Fifth Anniversary History of Temple Adath Israel, Lexington, Kentucky* (Lexington, Ky., 1979), p. 9; for Ashland, Harold Freedman letter, June 13, 1990.

13. Sonny Gergely of Harlan, telephone interview with author, Jan. 4, 1991.

14. Adath Israel Minute Book for 1903–09. See also Katz, ed., *Seventy Fifth Anniversary History*, pp. 5–7.

15. The earliest known written account of this tradition is in the Ohavay Zion Sisterhood yearbook for 1959.

16. On the founding of Keneseth Israel, the best published account is Landau, *Adath Louisville*, p. 56.

17. Richard Brown of Danville, letter to the author, Nov. 9, 1990; Lassetter, "Covington's Schule," pp. 23–25.

18. A good summary of the merger of Adath Israel and Brith Sholom, written very soon after the consolidation of the two congregations, is Landau, *Adath Louisville*, pp. 40–42.

19. See "New Congregation Leaves Merged Reform Temple" in *Louisville Courier-Journal*, Oct. 9, 1976.

20. For an interesting discussion of trends in intermarriage, see the published version of the first Belin Lecture in American Jewish Affairs at the University of Michigan: Egon Mayer, *A Demographic Revolution in American Jewry* (Ann Arbor, Mich., 1992).

21. See "Reform Group Organizes," *Community* (the newspaper of the Louisville Jewish Federation), Nov. 6, 1992; "Congregation Names Rabbi," *Community*, Dec. 18, 1992.

Chapter 2. Kentucky Synagogue Buildings

1. For an interesting ethnographic study of the internal dynamics of an Orthodox synagogue in contemporary America, see Samuel C. Heilman, *Synagogue Life: A Study in Symbolic Interaction* (Chicago, 1976).

2. Jonathan D. Sarna, "The Debate over Mixed Seating in the American Synagogue," in Wertheimer, *The American Synagogue*, p. 363.

3. See, for example, two clippings in the Adath Jeshurun archives (box 15, folder 1): "4 1/2–Acre Beard Estate to be Sold for $59,150 as Site for Synagogue," *Louisville Courier-Journal*, n.d. (c. 1951); and "Adath Jeshurun Starts Fund Drive for New Synagogue in Highlands," *Louisville Times*, Aug. 21, 1953.

4. Martin M. Perley, "A Short History of Congregation B'rith Sholom," in *Dedication Service: Congregation B'rith Sholom* (Louisville, 1956); Congregation Adath Jeshurun, *Special Messenger* (July 1955), p. 2 (copy in Adath Jeshurun archives, box 15, folder 1).

5. See Gary A. Tobin and Gabriel Berger, *The Jewish Community Federation of Louisville Demographic and Attitudinal Study* (Waltham, Mass., 1991), pp. 27–28.

Chapter 3. The First Century of Synagogue Design

1. See Albert S. Gottlieb, "Synagogue Architecture: Can a Purely Jewish Style Be Developed in the Building of Our Temples?" *American Hebrew*, April 14, 1916; and Gottlieb, "Synagogue Architecture: Past and Future," *American Hebrew*, April 11, 1919.

2. Lewis Mumford, "Towards a Modern Synagog Architecture," *Menorah Journal* 11 (June 1925): 230.

3. Ben Casseday, *The History of Louisville from its Earliest Settlement till the Year 1852* (Louisville, 1852), p. 216.

4. Quoted in Jacob Rader Marcus, *Memoirs of American Jews, 1775–1865*, 2: 75.

5. Bernheim, *History of the Settlement of Jews*, pp. 65–66.

6. Goldsmith, "History of Congregation Adath Israel," p. 16; Bernheim, *History of the Settlement of Jews*, p. 67.

7. This discussion is based primarily on material in the Bradshaw file at the Louisville Landmarks Commission.

8. Michael A. Meyer, *Response to Modernity: A History of the Reform Movement in Judaism* (New York, 1988), p. 183.

9. See Claxton Wilstach, ed., *Paducah and the Jackson Purchase in Kentucky* (Paducah, Ky., 1894), s.v. "Temple Israel"; Jonathan Jeffrey, "The Hill Builder: Brinton B. Davis and Western Kentucky University" (unpublished manuscript, c. 1992); Jonathan Jeffrey, letter to the author, n.d. (1992).

10. Minute Book of the Building and Finance Committee of K.K. Adas Israel for 1866–76, on deposit at The Temple, Louisville.

11. Edward Jamilly, "The Architecture of the Contemporary Synagogue," in Cecil Roth, ed., *Jewish Art: An Illustrated History*, rev. ed. by Bezalel Narkiss (Greenwich, Conn.: 1971), p. 274.

12. See William G. Tachau, "The Architecture of the Synagogue," *American Jewish Year Book* for 5687 (1926–27).

13. These discussions of McDonald, Sheblessy, Dodd, and Cobb are based primarily on Marty Lyn Poynter Hedgepeth, "The Victorian and the Beaux-Arts" (M.A. thesis, University of Louisville, 1981).

14. Typescript of speech dated Sept. 7, 1906, on deposit at The Temple, Louisville.

15. Mumford, "Towards a Modern Synagog Architecture," pp. 232–33.

16. Minutes of Dec. 2, 1917, in Adath Jeshurun Minute Book of 1911–22, in Adath Jeshurun archives, Louisville. The discussion of Gaffney's career is based primarily on materials in the Gaffney file at the Louisville Landmarks Commission.

17. "Death Claims L. K. Frankel," obituary in *Lexington Herald*, Nov. 28, 1949; C. Julian Oberwarth, *A History of the Profession of Architecture in Kentucky*, ed. William B. Scott, Jr. (Louisville, c. 1987), passim.

Chapter 4. Synagogue Design since World War II

1. Avram Kampf, *Contemporary Synagogue Art: Developments in the United States, 1945–1965* (New York, 1966), p. vii.

2. Ibid, p. 27.

3. Peter Blake, ed., *An American Synagogue for Today and Tomorrow: A Guide Book to Synagogue Design and Construction* (New York, 1954), pp. xiii, xiv, vii.

4. Kampf, *Contemporary Synagogue Art*, pp. 28–29.

5. Gerald Baron, architect of Temple Shalom, telephone interview with author, Sept. 3, 1992.

6. See Kampf, *Contemporary Synagogue Art*, pp. 46ff. "What Makes a Miracle?" *Journal of the Interfaith Forum on Religion, Art, and Architecture*, Spring 1984, pp. 28–29.

7. For a rare study of how one congregation chose an architect in the 1940s, see George M. Goodwin, "The Design of a Modern Synagogue: Percival Good-

man's Beth-El in Providence, Rhode Island," *American Jewish Archives* 45 (Spring-Summer, 1993).

8. "Information Concerning Proposed New Temple and Program of a Competition for the Selection of an Architect to Build Same," typescript, July 27, 1904, on deposit at The Temple, Louisville.

9. Rachel Wischnitzer-Bernstein "The Problem of Synagogue Architecture: Creating a Style Expressive of America," *Commentary* 3 (March 1947): 240–41.

10. See "Leslie Moss, Architect, Dies; Services Thursday," obituary in *Cincinnati Enquirer*, April 6, 1966.

11. See Katz, Seventy Fifth Anniversary History; and "Death Claims L.K. Frankel."

12. Minutes of Aug. 10 and Oct. 12, 1976, in Minute Book of Adath Israel for 1975–1979, on deposit at The Temple, Louisville.

13. *The Messenger* (newsletter of congregation Adath Jeshurun), Dec. 1954, p. 1.

14. Robert Nolan, Sr., architect of Keneseth Israel, telephone interview with author, Sept. 3, 1992.

15. Steve Caller of Ohavay Zion, letter to the author, May 5, 1992.

16. Gerald Baron, interview; Robert Nolan, Sr., interview.

17. Richard Wolf of The Temple, interview with author, Sept. 20, 1992.

18. Ibid.; Steve Caller letter.

19. Minutes for Oct. 12, 1905, and April 19, 1906, of the Adath Israel Committee on Site and Building, on deposit at The Temple, Louisville.

20. Carl J. Epping, of Gaffney and Epping, letter to M. Switow of Adath Jeshurun, Dec. 13, 1922, in the Adath Jeshurun archives (box 13, folder 3).

21. On the Roth sculpture controversy, see correspondence of 1957–59 between Adath Jeshurun and Sigmund Braverman in the Adath Jeshurun archives (box 15, folder 4); and "Symbol on Synagogue Poses Burning Enigma," *Louisville Courier-Journal*, April 5, 1957.

22. See correspondence of 1906–1908 between Harry Goodhue and Rabbi H.G. Enelow, on deposit at The Temple, Louisville.

23. Rabbi Solomon Roodman of Anshei Sfard, telephone interview with author, June 5, 1992.

24. See "Rediscovering Jewish Infrastructure: The Legacy of U.S. 19th Century Synagogues," *American Jewish History* 75 (1986).

Discovering Kentucky's Synagogues

1. *Dedication: Keneseth Israel Congregation* (Louisville, 1971), p. 17; Landau, *Adath Louisville*, p. 55; "Handsome Synagogue Dedicated by B'nai Jacob Congregation," *Louisville Courier-Journal*, March 25, 1901.

2. Th. David, "Snopsis [*sic*] of the History of the Jews of the City of Louisville, Kentucky" (c. 1876), manuscript at the American Jewish Historical Society, Waltham, Mass. (Board of Delegates of American Israelites manuscript collection, box 4); William Henry Perrin, ed., *History of Fayette County, Kentucky* (Chicago, 1882), p. 336; Jacob J. Polish, report on Middlesboro, Ky. (1935), on deposit at the American Jewish Archives, Cincinnati (box 2259).

3. *American Israelite*, March 4, 1881; *Historical Churches of Daviess County* (Owensboro, Ky., 1976), s.v. "Temple Adath Israel"; booklet prepared for the Bittman Bat Mitzvah celebration (1984).

4. See *History of Daviess County, Kentucky* (Chicago, 1883; reprinted Evansville, Ind., 1966), p. 385; William Foster Hayes, *Sixty Years of Owensboro, 1883–1943* (Owensboro, Ky., c. 1943), pp. 212–13; "Yom Kippur Celebration Begins Today," *Owensboro Messenger and Inquirer*, Sept. 17, 1972.

5. Goldsmith, "History of Congregation Adath Israel," p. 13; "Temple Adath Israel to Celebrate Anniversary," *Louisville Courier-Journal*, Jan. 12, 1918.

6. Josiah Stoddard Johnston, *Memorial History of Louisville from Its First Settlement to the Year 1896* (Chicago, 1896), 2: 276; *American Jewish Year Book* for 5668 (1907–08), p. 183; *Dedication: Keneseth Israel Congregation*, p. 17; Landau, *Adath Louisville*, p. 55.

7. Morris Weintraub, former president of the United Hebrew Congregation, letter to the author, August 28, 1990.

8. For a good commentary on the importance of nineteenth-century bird's-eye-view maps, see John W. Reps, *Views and Viewmakers of Urban America: Lithographs of Towns and Cities in the U.S. and Canada . . . 1825–1925* (Columbia, Mo., 1984).

Index

Index